CARRY ON

A 30-Day Devotional to Encourage You to See God in Everyday Life

Carry On!!!

D. L. Wood

David L. Wood
Author of Pieces of My Heart

Carry On

A 30-Day Devotional That Encourages You to See God in Your Everyday Life

David L. Wood © 2022

This author and publisher supports copyright. Copyright fuels creativity, encourages diverse voices, promotes free speech, and creates a vibrant culture. Thank you for buying an authorized edition of this book and for complying with copyright laws by not reproducing, scanning, or distributing any part of it in any form without permission.

While the publisher and author have used their best efforts in preparing this book, they make no representations or warranties with respect to the accuracy or completeness of this book and specifically disclaim any implied warranties of merchantability or fitness for a particular purpose. No warranty may be created or extended by sales representatives or written sales materials. The advice and strategies contained herein may not be suitable for your situation. You should consult with a professional where appropriate. The stories and interviews in this book are true although the names and identifiable information may have been changed to maintain confidentiality.

The publisher and author shall have neither liability nor responsibility to any person or entity with respect to loss, damage, or injury caused or alleged to be caused directly or indirectly by the information contained in this book. The information presented herein is in no way intended as a substitute for counseling or other professional guidance.

All Bible verses are from the 2011 New International Version (NIV).

Print ISBN: 979-8-9861415-0-3

Printed in the United States of America

Dedication

First, I would like to dedicate this book to my Heavenly Father, my Lord and Savior, Jesus and my teacher, comforter and counselor, the Holy Spirit of God. Without God working in my life, there would be no first book, no second book, and no books in the future. Make no mistake, everything good in my life, I owe to God. EVERYTHING!

I would also like to dedicate this book to my wife of 33 years, Denice. Her love, dedication, and grace to me are beyond words of gratitude to express. She has believed in me when I did not believe in myself. She saw past my flaws and shortcomings and saw all the way to the man God is making me to be. God is the Author and Finisher of our faith and He blessed me with the best partner to walk through this life with, and I am so thankful.

I would like to dedicate this book to my six daughters. I am so proud to be able to call you all my daughters. I am so proud of the loving, caring, and quality-filled young women you have become, and I am also so happy to see God working in all of your lives in various ways.

Lastly, I would like to dedicate this book to my 12 grandchildren. I look forward to all that God has for you as you walk your journey in this fun thing we call . . . life. Along with all of you, I am excited to leave something of myself behind for my great-grandkids, as well as my great-great-grandkids, and even my great-great-great grandkids. I think you get the picture. My prayer for every one of you is that all your life journeys lead you right to the ONE who knows you the best and loves you the most.

CONTENTS

How to Use This Book		9
Introduction		11
Day 1:	Papa Loves You	13
Day 2:	A Tale of Two Tails	17
Day 3:	The Offense on the Fence	21
Day 4:	A Changing Tide	29
Day 5:	Second Chance Popcorn	35
Day 6:	I Could Have Had a V8	41
Day 7:	A Perspective Made of Tears	47
Day 8:	Come Hither, Heather	55
Day 9:	The Great Conductor	59
Day 10:	A Batty Perspective	63
Day 11:	One Leg in, One Leg Out	73
Day 12:	A Grizzly Business Deal	79
Day 13:	Floppy Bags	85
Day 14:	Getting in the Groove	91
Day 15:	Burnt Toast	97
Day 16:	The Construction of Life	101
Day 17:	Sink or Swim	107
Day 18:	The Making of Kitty Wampus	113
Day 19:	Go Fly a Kite	121
Day 20:	Rolling With De Papa	127
Day 21:	One Bun or Two?	133

Day 22: The Source of Course	141
Day 23: Knock, Knock . . . Who's There?	145
Day 24: Milking It	151
Day 25: Don't Be Alarmed	155
Day 26: The Hubcaps of Life	163
Day 27: Spider Defense	169
Day 28: Winging It	175
Day 29: The Trouble With Stubble	183
Day 30: Twelve Horned Toads, One Mean Lizard, and an Earthquake	191
Acknowledgments	198
About the Author	199

How to Use This Book

What am I supposed to do with this book? What is a 30-day devotional? What if I start in February? what will happen to two extra days? Is Sasquatch real or not? Does the light really go off when you close the refrigerator door? All of these questions are fantastic. But let me answer the ones about this devotional. I will do my best to answer the rest some other time.

I hope that this 30-day devotional will be a super-duper spectacularly awesome tool that will help you focus on God and start your day off in a great and wonderfully positive direction. That is my high expectation for this book. The truth is, how great this book can be completely depends on the user. And that my friend, is you.

The key is to first set a date to start reading this book and commit to it. Next, pick a time to read it that you are most likely to be successful on a daily basis. For me, that is early in the morning, before the world wakes up and starts getting crazy and demanding. Once you find that time, start your first day and read the story. Think about how and if you can relate to what you have read and maybe jot down a few notes about that. Read

A 30-Day Devotional

the focus question and pray the prayer. As you do this, feel free to make it your own. Add your observations and feelings into it as you talk to the One who knows you the best and loves you the most. Take a little time to reflect and then go out and make it a good day.

Tomorrow morning, just like your shampoo, rinse and repeat. That's all there is to it.

Introduction

Who is this "David L. Wood" anyway, and why do I want to read his book? Is he some rich and famous actor? Is he a professional athlete with a lucrative Nike advertising contract? Is he some Instagram or TikTok sensation with twelve million followers? Is he some highly educated man with degrees hanging all over his wall or maybe a brain surgeon that saves lives on a daily basis? No, David L. Wood is none of those things. David L. Wood is simply . . . me.

He is just a guy who works way too hard for a living, loves his family, and loves God. He is someone who has been through the good times and been though the bad. He has spent time on the mountain tops as well as the deep valleys this life can bring. He has rode the rollercoaster of life though ups and downs and all arounds. Life has been very hard in some situations and extremely kind others. And he is someone who has learned to see God in the midst of it all. And if you are not any of the people described in the first paragraph, you just might find David L. Wood is very much like you. And that is exactly why you just might want to read what he has to say. Because I think you might just relate.

A 30-Day Devotional

Carry On is the first book in the planned Current View series. These 30-day devotions will aim to share the lessons that are all around us each and every day. It is my hope that reading about my current view of God working in my life will inspire you to find your own current view of God working in yours. That maybe, it will cause you to stop and notice just how much God is actually doing all around you and me, even when we are too busy to notice. And in doing so, you will discover the One that knows you the best and loves you the most, in a whole new interactive way and even gain strength to help you.

Day 1

Papa Loves You

This morning I went through my normal routine. I woke up to my alarm, unplugged my phone, and went into the bathroom. Then I went back out and picked up my dog's bed, with her inside it like I do every morning, and brought her into the bathroom with me. Peanut tends to not sleep much once I get up, so to keep her from waking up my wife, I just take her with me to remove the chance of that. She will usually sleep, and then wake up to scratch a few times and then doze back off until I am ready.

Most mornings after I am ready, I have a little quiet/prayer time in the closet and about 50% of the time Peanut will come in to join me. She is not there to pray though, but rather to coax me into petting her.

When I am done, I toss her bed back in its place and we head downstairs where I let her out the sliding glass door to do her business. Usually, she hears me getting her food and comes back in her dog door. If it is too quick, I just send her back out again for a second try. When she comes back in, I am usually getting her food ready. She has lost a few teeth, so I put hot water on her food and stir it with my finger to soften it up a bit for her. My wife, Denice, gives me a hard time about this, but I really have compassion for Peanut and her extra gum space.

Peanut is a little strange and really loves veggies. Each morning I will give her at least a leaf of lettuce, breaking it up into bite size pieces for her. I think her love of these treats is cool and should be very good for her and "ruff . . . ruff . . . ruffage" consumption must be a good thing.

My family often accuses me of spoiling Peanut, but I have no idea what they are talking about. I think they are just jealous, to tell you the truth.

Anyway, before I leave, I will usually clip on her collar, pet her and scratch her favorite spots, and tell her to have a good day. Then like normal as I am moving for the door, I tell her, "Papa loves you."

I had not really given it a second thought before, but this morning when I said that, a thought immediately came into my head. "You have a Papa that loves you too." The thought was clear and loud and rang as simply . . . truth.

Peanut is a grouchy, snappy, quick-to-anger kind of a dog. And yet there is no doubt in her mind that she is loved by me in all her shortcomings. And just like Peanut, I can be grouchy, snappy, and quick-to-anger. Actually, I can make much bigger mistakes than that and have throughout my life. I am a mess at times and in need of renovation. I am undeserving of having our Great Papa love me. Yet He does—more than I can imagine. Having a relationship with us was worth the pain, suffering, and sacrifice of His only Son. That is huge and way beyond my understanding. I mean, I know me, and I would not have ever considered doing that for me. But yet, He did.

I think He must see me for who I will be one day instead of who I am now, for whom He has made me to be instead of who I have made me to be. All I know for sure is that my loving Father loves me in spite of me and all my faults. And He loves each and every

Papa Loves You

one of us with that same great love and longs to be in a close loving relationship with us.

So, as you start this day, please hear these words crisply and clearly . . . "Papa loves you!"

Father, Thank You for loving me no matter how I am feeling or who I'm barking at. Thank You for always being there to take care of me.

Love,

David

Romans 5:8

But God demonstrates his own love for us in this: While we were still sinners, Christ died for us.

How would your life change if you remembered that Papa loves you always?

Day 2
A Tale of Two Tails

As I was eating oatmeal at the kitchen table this morning, I looked over at a box that my wife, Denice, had put on the table while she was taking inventory of her doTERRA oils. On the box it read, "Retail." As I looked and read that word, this thought came to mind. RE + TAIL = to put a tail back on again. This logically and pragmatically led to me seeing a picture of Eeyore in my mind.

There he was in my mind with his pessimistic attitude, and I could hear him saying, "Well, it's not much of a tail." And it was that tail that had my interest. It was a tale of a tail I tell you, that I thought I must try to tell. How it will turn out there is no telling.

Have you noticed that Eeyore's tail is held on by a nail? By a nail. We don't know much about why that is, do we? Sometime, somewhere, somehow, Eeyore had been re-tailed. Something dreadful (to use Pooh language) had happened to poor Eeyore, ripping his tail clean off! (Which may help explain his disposition a little.)

If I had a tail (which I don't . . . don't believe the mean rumors) and it was ripped clean off my body and then someone put it back on with a nail, I think the chances of me having a bad attitude would be high—especially every time I sat down. And with that thought . . . why don't we know more about this matter?

I would tell everyone what had happened to my tail if I had lost it, but with Eeyore, nothing is explained. We are just supposed to go along, not asking any questions, pretending like all donkeys have their tails held on with a nail. And thinking about the last four words . . . "Held on with a nail" . . . ouch, that can't feel good either, even if you are just an animated character. And just like me in my imagination above, another possible reason for his disposition.

You see, we really don't know much about Eeyore's past and why he is how he is. We just see him in the whole tail aftermath (WTA) and think of him as the donkey with the downer, pessimistic attitude. Maybe if there had been a book written before the Pooh series explaining about the life of Eeyore, we may feel completely differently about him. They could call it, "Eeyore . . . the Tale of a Missing Tail" or maybe "A Tell-All Tale about the Tail of a Donkey" or even "The Tail . . . No Tail, Tale" or possibly, "101 Ways to Nail on a Tail."

Maybe if we had this added perspective, we would think of Eeyore differently and maybe we would even see him as an over-comer with his nailed-on tail. Our new perspective may even change the way we interacted with Eeyore and that in turn may have a positive effect on how Eeyore interacted with us and those around him and even better . . . how he thought about himself. Indeed, that would be a great thing for sure.

It is a good thing that this story is just an animated example as we would never do anything like this in "real life." We would never treat real, flesh and blood people in this way. We would never judge a person by their appearance, attitude, education, or social status. That would just be so shallow of a perspective, wouldn't it? We are all aware that God has made every one of us and that we all have great value as His ultimate creation. And we are aware that behind every person there is a story that has

A Tale of Two Tails

brought them where they are today. And we always take the time to hear that story before we make assumptions because we are smart enough to know that we have not walked in their shoes. Yes, we all know much better than that, because we have learned that loving people is our highest calling in this life.

With that, have a blissful Winnie-the-Pooh day.

Daddy, I thank You so much that you see past all the things I try to hide behind in this life. I thank You that You know everything about me . . . all the places I have been, where I am going and everything that makes me who I am today. I thank You that You have loved me my whole life, even when I can't or could not love myself. Please continue to try to show me how to love like You. That would be such an awesome gift to me and to those You have blessed me with in this life.

Love,

David

1 Samuel 16:7

But the Lord said to Samuel, "Do not consider his appearance or his height, for I have rejected him. The Lord does not look at the things people look at. People look at the outward appearance, but the Lord looks at the heart."

Psalm 139:13-16

For you created my inmost being; you knit me together in my mother's womb. I praise you because I am fearfully and wonderfully made; your works are wonderful, I know that full well. My frame was not hidden from you when I was made in the secret place, when I was woven together in the depths of the earth. Your eyes saw my unformed body; all the days ordained for me were written in your book before one of them came to be.

1 Corinthians 13:1-3

If I speak in the tongues of men or of angels, but do not have love, I am only a resounding gong or a clanging cymbal. If I have the gift of prophecy and can fathom all mysteries and all knowledge, and if I have a faith that can move mountains, but do not have love, I am nothing. If I give all I possess to the poor and give over my body to hardship that I may boast, but do not have love, I gain nothing.

How would remembering that everyone has past pain change the way you treat them?

Day 3
The Offense on the Fence

There I was, taking a walk with my wife in our neighborhood like I had done many times before. But on the way back home, something was different. I noticed a fence that had been broken apart in several places. The first two places were small, with only a few pickets knocked off, but the last place was much, much larger. It appeared to me that a car had probably hit some ice on the road and spun off, striking the fence a few times as it spun around. The largest hole with the missing pickets was the target of the biggest portion of the car.

Now this was an older fence that had obviously been around for a long time or maybe a fence that had just never been protected properly and had weathered badly. I can really relate to that some days, when I first get up in the morning and look in the mirror. Either way, it was very dried and dark and to try to repair this fence with new pickets would have looked tacky. That reminds me of the verse in the Bible talking about putting new wine in old wine skins. (Matthew 9:17, Mark 2:22, Luke 5:37)

Before the fence had been so rudely interrupted and broken apart, everything was fine and the fence was perfectly happy being what it was: old and in need of some attention, but nevertheless, still a fence. The owners probably never gave it a second look or thought until it was broken apart and required attention. It kept people out of their yard and gave them the privacy they were after, thus doing its job. With the fence intact, it had blocked the view of what went on behind it, but now, with big holes in it, what was behind was open to whoever happened to walk or drive by. And for the first time since living in this area and going on many walks past it, I saw that the yard behind the fence really was kind of neglected and maybe a little junky. In this way, I guess it matched the fence. If this had never happened to the fence, I and everyone driving and walking by would have been none the wiser. And, so it is with you and with me.

In this life, I think we build all kinds of fences in different ways. Some fences we build to keep people we deem "not safe" out and other fences I think we build to keep people that we consider "safe" in with us. We build different fences for work, home, church, and play. We may give certain people access to a gate to enter in and out of our fences, while others we just make sure we never let in.

Then I think we build fences inside our fences that offer certain people even more personal view and access to us. Kind of like a "Holy of Holies" place. Only the most trusted people can get access to this place. These people are the ones who have proven that they simply love us, despite all our faults and quirks. Not many people are granted access to that inner fence in most people's lives, but hopefully we all have someone who we trust that much.

I think some fences we build in life are healthy and necessary as they create healthy boundaries to help us and to protect us. To

The Offense on the Fence

let someone inside who could hurt us or who does not have our best interest in mind falls into the category of "giving dogs what is sacred or throwing your pearls to swine" and should be avoided. (Matt 7:6) So, we carefully consider each person in our lives to see just what kind of access they should get or if they should get any access at all.

There are also other fences that we build in our lives that are not healthy. These fences are built out of deep hurt, disappointment, anger, or fear. For example, someone who has been devastated and/or betrayed in a relationship might choose to build a big, bad fence around their heart. This fence may be accompanied by a wide, deep moat filled with piranhas, snapping turtles, ninja frogs with throwing stars, electric eels with flamethrowers, sharks with lasers on their heads, and alligators with long nails that they will use to scratch on chalkboards in unison if you come too close. Mr. T would say something like, "I pity the fool who would try to get over to that man or woman." This is not a job that even the A-Team would attempt, cool theme music or not!

It is the hope of this person that no one will ever get close enough to hurt them like that again. And although they may be successful, they have also isolated themselves from depth of life, causing them to voluntarily miss out on so much of what God has for them. We all know that the best, brightest, and biggest things in life also seem to carry the biggest risks. You simply cannot play it safe and experience the deepest and best God has for you at the same time.

I also think we have fenced-off areas in our lives that have been in place for so long that we may not even be aware that fences are even there. They have been there so long that they are dark and dried out and just seem to be a part of who we are. Some of your identity may even be built into these fences. You may not remember a time in your life when a particular fence was not standing. It may have been built long, long, ago, maybe even when you were a child. Even you may not know all that lies behind these fences or exactly why you built them in the first place. But "Someone" does and that "Someone" is your best source for sorting out what needs to be in your life as a boundary to protect you and what needs to come down so you can be free. And if you ask, He will help you.

Healthy fences that set boundaries in our lives are necessary with people, but when it comes to our relationship with God, there is no such thing as a healthy fence between God and us. In a perfect design it should look like this: "Godus." And yet we have built fences all over the place. We build new ones, when necessary, in hopes that the Creator of you and me will not peek over the top or between the pickets, or try to open the gates we have around areas we do not want to give Him access to. We do the "move along . . . nothing to see here . . . hey look, something shiny" kind of thing in hopes that we can just keep those parts all hidden and never have to deal with them. But there the King of kings stands, knocking on our gate. (Revelation 3:20) Knock, knock, knock . . . Knock, knock, knock . . . "David, can I come in?" *High voice* . . . "David is not here right now, Mr. Almighty . . . I think he went to church and is spending the night at the homeless shelter."

Have you ever prayed for God's will in your life? Have you ever said something like, "God, just show me what You want, and I will do it," or "Oh God, please give me direction," or "Jesus, I want to serve You and I want what You want for my life," or "God, what do You want from me?" or simply "Please show me the way?" Maybe it is just me, but I have often said things very much like these and then struggled against God when He began to try to show me. Geesh, I am so hopeless and clueless on my own.

"Something" knocks one of your pickets off. You stop and say, "Hey, what is up with that?" as you nail it back on. "God, please show me the direction You want me to go," . . . and two pickets come flying off. You quickly scurry to pick them up and throw in an emergency 9-1-1 prayer. "God, I am being attacked here . . .

The Offense on the Fence

hello?!? Don't You see what is going on here? Please help me!!!" God nods in an affirmative direction and then, WHAM!!! A huge section of your fence is torn from your life, breaking off the 2x4s at ground level and exposing areas you are not comfortable with being out in the open. As you frantically try to gather pieces to nail and lean back into place, you hear a voice say,

"David, stop. Lay it down." "But God, my fence is lying all over the place. Please help me." And He says, "I JUST DID."

God is all about our freedom. He does not want there to be any areas in our lives that hold us back and more importantly, that keep us at a distance from Him. He wants our trust to be in Him and in Him first and ultimately. He wants the areas that keep us hidden and superficial to be torn down and replaced with the openness and depth that He made us to live in. In short, He wants us to always be moving closer to Him and He wants us to be real, living in authenticity. His will, His purpose, His plan, are all wrapped up in nothing less than the very best that He has for our lives. His will still is and has always been, to be closerthanthis to us. He gave His only Son to make this all possible. But the choice is still always ours. If we allow Him to, He will tear down the things that need to go away and He, the maker of everything we know, the very One who positioned the planets and strung the stars in the sky, will begin to rebuild our lives from the ash and the rubble. The old will be no more and He will be our foundation.

Will it be painful? Yes. It will probably be profoundly painful! Will it be hard? Yes, it will—extremely, tremendously hard! But remember that nothing of great value and worth in this life comes out of ease. What I believe with all my heart is that no matter what it costs, no matter how painful the process, no matter how deep the sorrow, in the end when it is all over, the sun and Son will break through and will shine again and it will be totally worth the journey.

My Father, there are so many areas in my life that need You to do the "Home Makeover" thingy to. I desperately need You this moment and I personally invite You now to come into my life and demolish anything and everything that distances me from You and that keeps me from being who You made me to be. Rebuild me and make me into something totally pleasing in Your sight.

I love you,

David

Matthew 9:17

"Neither do men pour new wine into old wineskins. If they do, the skins will burst, the wine will run out and the wineskins will be ruined. No, they pour new wine into new wineskins, and both are preserved."

Matthew 7:6

Do not give dogs what is sacred; do not throw your pearls to pigs. If you do, they may trample them under their feet, and then turn and tear you to pieces.

Revelation 3:20

Here I am! I stand at the door and knock. If anyone hears my voice and opens the door, I will come in and eat with him, and he with me.

The Offense on the Fence

Psalm 127:1a

Unless the LORD builds the house, its builders labor in vain.

What fences have you built to keep people out? What would life look like if you removed those fences?

Day 4
A Changing Tide

As I walked along the seashore in Pismo Beach, California, the sound of the ocean was soothing as the waves were coming in and going out. I tried to take a walk every morning before going and starting my visits with my two daughters and four of my grandchildren that live in that area. Like normal, as I walked along, my eyes were scanning the sand for shells that caught my attention.

This morning, I was also aware of all the prints that were in the sand. There was evidence that I was not the first person to walk on the sand today. There were many other footprints of various sizes as well. Many different dog prints and various other prints (pony, zebra, koala bear, elephant, monkey, lemur, three-legged alligator, snail, and a caterpillar with one wooden leg) going in every direction and my feet were making the newest prints as I walked along leaving evidence that I had been there too (along with the other people, critters, and whatnot).

A 30-Day Devotional

Then the thought occurred to me that if I had been the first one on the beach today, there would not have been any other prints at all, because the waves would have washed them all away overnight, clearing the beach of all that had happened on it before the high tide. It had, in its own way, cleaned the slate of all activity from before that point. We could say that the sand on the beach starts out new every morning.

That thought brought me quickly to the reminder of what God has done for us in removing all our sins with the tide of His Son's blood. In the beginning, when we first said, "Yes," to His gift of salvation, all our footprints, all our selfish paths and wasted rabbit trails we had made on our own were wiped clean—washed away if you will. From that point on, as we work out our new way of life in Christ, when we don't get it quite right, we can bring those mistakes and lay them at the feet of Jesus. And as we do that, in comes the tide of Christ's love into our lives covering all that was there before and when it goes back out, all the missteps are long gone, just like the smooth fresh sand on the beach shining in the new morning dawn. And best of all, the Word says that God remembers them no more. We usually remember them, but the Word tells us that as far as God is concerned, they never happened.

It was a sweet analogy as I reflected on this visual reminder of God's great love and forgiveness for us, His children.

On my walk back from the pier and to the hotel, another lesson began to form as I searched and found some shells to take with me.

I decided that I wanted to find some sand dollars. Even though most of them were broken, each one had parts that still had a beautiful design on them, despite the abuse they had taken. Some were missing the tops while others were missing the bottom. Still others were broken into various pieces. I chose three of them.

A Changing Tide

One was almost a full sand dollar that still showed most of the star-like design on the top, but it was worn hard around the edges. The other two were ones that were broken in half. Even though they both had major damage, they possessed great beauty on the parts that were still there. They were literally "shells" of their original selves, yet, they were still very much sand dollars and valuable to me.

The same tide that cleared the sand was also responsible for a lot of the wear and tear on the shells I was looking at. Plus, many were also damaged from being trampled on by all the people, dogs, and critters walking around.

This reminds me of life as I have known it. This life has given me a lot through the years, but at the same time it has also taken much from me and has been very hard on me. I have lost large pieces of myself along the way as the tide of life has come in and gone out, leaving me worn and battered. I have also been broken in many places by people, situations, and circumstances that trampled me down—leaving me broken. Have you been there? I think most of us have.

But God, the creator of the universe saw value in me. With all my pieces missing and all my broken areas exposed, He saw value in me. And He has picked me up over and over, even when I was where I was due to my own freewill and walking into where I know He did not want me to go. Yet even then, when I cried for mercy, He was always there to pick me up, brush me off, and help me get walking on my feet again and out of the wrong turn I had taken.

That same God that picked me up so many times is also the same One that is there for you. He is waiting for you to call on Him, waiting for you to let Him smooth the sand of your missteps in life and take the brokenness you have experienced and make it into something beautiful. The question is: Will you let Him?

A 30-Day Devotional

Father, You have been so good to me. You have been faithful always, even though I have often not been faithful to You. Your love has been the only truly steady thing throughout my life from the time I was born until present and yet, I have often taken it for granted. Your compassion and love for me are truly new every morning and this day, I am so thankful and grateful for all You have done for me. Please use me, teach me, lead me, and guide me. Help me to be who You made me to be. Show me the way.

Love,

David

Lamentations 3:22-23

Because of the Lord's great love we are not consumed, for his compassions never fail. They are new every morning; great is your faithfulness.

Psalm 103:11-18

For as high as the heavens are above the earth, so great is his love for those who fear him; as far as the east is from the west, so far has he removed our transgressions from us. As a father has compassion on his children, so the Lord has compassion on those who fear him; for he knows how we are formed, he remembers that we are dust. The life of mortals is like grass, he flourishes like a flower of the field; the wind blows over it and it is gone, and its place remembers it no more. But from everlasting to everlasting the Lord's love is with those who fear him, and his righteousness with their children's children—with those who keep his covenant and remember to obey his precepts.

A Changing Tide

Jeremiah 31:34

No longer will they teach their neighbor, or say to one another, 'Know the Lord,' because they will all know me, from the least of them to the greatest," declares the Lord. "For I will forgive their wickedness and will remember their sins no more."

Isaiah 43:25

I, even I, am he who blots out your transgressions, for my own sake, and remembers your sins no more.

Isaiah 61:1-3

The Spirit of the Sovereign Lord is on me, because the Lord has anointed me to preach good news to the poor. He has sent me to bind up the brokenhearted, to proclaim freedom for the captives and release from darkness for the prisoners, to proclaim the year of the Lord's favor and the day of vengeance of our God, to comfort all who mourn, and provide for those who grieve in Zion—to bestow on them a crown of beauty instead of ashes, the oil of joy instead of mourning, and a garment of praise instead of a spirit of despair. They will be called oaks of righteousness, a planting of the Lord for the display of his splendor.

Do you have footprints in your life that the Lord needs to wash away? Are you at a place in your life where you can ask the Lord to show you the beauty of your brokenness?

Day 5

Second-Chance Popcorn

Some people have what is referred to as a "sweet tooth" but my wife has a "popcorn tooth." She loves real, fresh popcorn (not the microwave kind). Her brand preference is Orville Redenbacher's gourmet popcorn (ORGP for future reference) popped in a hot-air popcorn popper. She does not put butter on it but only salt, so it is not too unhealthy as snacks go, especially when compared to anything with "Little Debbie" in front of it. We have been out of her favorite brand for a couple of weeks and she has been starting to go through withdrawals. We rented a movie a week ago and they had microwave popcorn in the checkout which I pointed out to her. She is very loyal to her hot-air popper popcorn and would not accept the cheap substitute. But last night was her night.

After a trip to Costco, she once again had her beloved supply of ORGP and filled the pre-measured container of the hot-air popcorn popper and plugged it into the wall and waited for some delicious popcorn delight (DPD for future reference). In a matter of seconds, the white fluffy popcorn began to fill the awaiting container. After a few minutes the sound of newly transformed popcorn had ceased and there were no more clinking sounds of untransformed popcorn left in the hot-air popper.

At this point, my wife pulled the plug from the wall and started emptying her harvest from the container into the waiting white bowl where she applied the salt, while sampling a few as she dumped. It was then that she said to me, "Wow, there are sure a lot of old maids for gourmet popcorn."

I said, "Say what?" She repeated herself and then asked if I had heard that term before. She was referring to the un-popped or as I referred to them earlier, untransformed popcorn. I had not heard that saying used for popcorn but knew what she was talking about and realized why they were called that when she said it.

In examining the bottom of the container, I observed that there was truly a lot of untransformed popcorn left in the container, way more than I would have expected. I expected a minimal amount due to the ones getting taken from the heat along with transformed popcorn flying out, but I did not expect many duds ... especially not from ORGP. But there they were, much to my dismay ... hundreds of them it seemed. (On a side note, I had to scoop and count the approximate amount of popcorn that goes into the popper. Just to show how anal I am, there were 724.)

This did not sit well with me and I asked my wife why she did not put them back through. She said she had never done this because she thought that if they did not pop the first time through, they were not going to pop. She then commented they might burn but that I could try if I wanted to. Well, that was all I needed to hear ... yes, I wanted to!!!

Putting on my best superhero attitude and imaginary tights, I went back through all the untransformed popcorn. I put them

Second-Chance Popcorn

all back into the hot-air popper, plugged it back into the wall and subjected them once again to the heat. A few of them came flying out again right away and after about thirty seconds passed, I thought that maybe my wife was right and I was wasting my time. But then it happened. POP . . . out came a big white fluffy guy with a big smile on his popcorn face. Then there was another and then another and another and then finally . . . silence.

At this I was exuberant and brought the container into my wife exclaiming, "Here is your second chance popcorn!" Then I put them all in with the other popcorn.

About half of them have transformed during this second run, so I gathered the rest for another try. Again, with a little more heat, more white fluffy happy guys and gals came flying out smiling and giggling until again there was silence.

This cycle continued over and over again until I was down to trying to grab the last 20 or so with my fingers, continually throwing them back in to the heat as they would fly out untransformed while I yelled at the top of my lungs, "COME ON LITTLE GUYS AND GALS, YOU CAN DO IT!" This did not go so well as the little suckers were hot and caused me to make small yelping sounds from the pain they were inflicting on my fingertips. I quickly regrouped and knew I had to go to "Plan B" . . . a spoon. With this spoon, I continued over and over to scoop the untransformed kernels back into the heat until I was down to only about four left in their untransformed state. At this point, I called the experiment done and, "A GREAT SUCCESS FOR POPCORN WORLDWIDE." (AGSFPW for future reference)

Have you ever felt the heat? You know what I am talking about—that searing heat of the Holy Spirit of God trying to "POP" something in your life? It starts at our conversion, when we are born again: "POP." And it continues as God challenges us to grow and mature.

A 30-Day Devotional

Some of us initially pop when we are very young, some of us years later when we are a little older. Some of us pop when we are teens and some of us in our 20s and 30s. Some of us stubborn ones pop at a much older age and a few of us . . . never pop. But it's not because God was not giving us what we needed to pop or pursuing us throughout our lives. Like the parable about the shepherd going after his lost sheep, so our Father is always looking to bring us home.

If I wanted to put a corn pun here, I would suggest that God even has "stalked" us throughout our lives and tried to show us that we "reap what we sow," but I am not interested in inserting "corny" lines just to get a few more "ears" listening to this story. So just forget it, it's not going to happen. You are just going to have to wait for a whole other "crop" of words if you are looking for that kind of "harvest." Sorry, this is just not the right place to or time to "plant" some puns.

You see, we have the free will to keep jumping in OR out of the hot-air popper, so to speak. From our initial conversion to new life, to every opportunity for growth God brings our way, we have the ability to keep rejecting the truth. To reject the next step is to reject and step out of the heat. God will continue to pursue us until the very end of our lives. He is the God of first chances and the God of second chances. He is also the God of third, fourth and fifth chances. How high can you count? He is the God of that many chances until the very end. He will continue to spoon feed you back into the Holy Spirit air popper in hopes that you will finally say, "YES" to the best He has for you.

Think about a few of these examples: Peter, from his triple-denying of Jesus to becoming a great pillar of the church. Saul/Paul, from persecutor of the church to servant of the Lord, great teacher and church planter who wrote the bulk of the New Testament. Woman caught in adultery, from certain death by stoning to forgiveness and a new start. Rahab, from prostitute to savior of Joshua's spies and into the bloodline of Christ. Mary Magdalene, from a woman possessed by seven demons to a

Second-Chance Popcorn

devout and delivered follower of Christ. YOU and ME, from "_____" to "_____." How would you fill in these blanks? Where do you still need to pop? The choice is up to you. The GREAT AIR POPPER is waiting.

Father . . . my Potter, it's me, Your clay. Your stubborn and fickle clay. I do not understand why You love me so much that You would come after me to bring me home. I do not understand why You continue to try to refine me when at times getting me to listen is like trying to nail Jell-O to a wall. But what I do know is I am so grateful for Your love and faithfulness. Thank You dear Father for never, ever giving up on me. You are amazing.

I love you,

David

Luke 15:3-7

Then Jesus told them this parable: "Suppose one of you has a hundred sheep and loses one of them. Doesn't he leave the ninety-nine in the open country and go after the lost sheep until he finds it? And when he finds it, he joyfully puts it on his shoulders and goes home. Then he calls his friends and neighbors together and says, 'Rejoice with me; I have found my lost sheep.' I tell you that in the same way there will be more rejoicing in heaven over one sinner who repents than over ninety-nine righteous persons who do not need to repent."

Isaiah 64:8

Yet you, Lord, are our Father. We are the clay, you are the potter; we are all the work of your hand.

Psalm 12:6

And the words of the Lord are flawless, like silver refined in a crucible, like gold refined seven times.

Psalm 66:10

For you, God, tested us; you refined us like silver.

Isaiah 48:10

See, I have refined you, though not as silver; I have tested you in the furnace of affliction.

Jeremiah 9:7

Therefore this is what the Lord Almighty says: "See, I will refine and test them, for what else can I do because of the sin of my people?"

How would you fill in these blanks of where you were before being transformed by Christ to where you are now? In what areas do you still need to pop?

Day 6
I Could Have Had a V8

As I was getting ready to ride my motorcycle to work this morning, I slipped two V8s into my motorcycle jacket, one in the left pocket and one in the right. As I zipped the pockets shut, a thought ran through my brain (I know . . . scary). I thought, if I were to get into an accident, the V8s will surely rupture and if I was unconscious, I will look like a goner to the paramedics.

Coming up on the scene, it would look very gruesome no doubt. First, just because of how old I am getting and the all the things gravity has pulled from their God-given places, it may gross out a high percentage of the first responders. But then added on top of that, seeing all the V8 oozing through the whole front of the belly of my motorcycle jacket, that would be the last straw for a few more. I'm sure it would be more than the average emergency personnel would want to see, especially right after an all-you-can-eat-spaghetti-feed at the station that day.

A 30-Day Devotional

Following that line of thought in a logical manner, I imagined what would happen next would be the scene of me waking up in the morgue, realizing what had just happened. I'm sure there would be panic in my eyes that were the size of saucers and that my high-pitched squeal yelling, "HELLO, IT'S ONLY V8 ... I'M NOT DEAD HERE," would attract some attention.

I'm sure the coroner at that point would enter through the double doors with a ham sandwich in his left hand with three bites missing and ask, "Sir, what do you mean you're not dead? I have a paper right here that says you are very dead. Do you have one that says that you are NOT dead?"

At this I would sit up, swing my legs over the side of the metal gurney and respond, "Well no, I do not happen to carry that with me at all times, but I could run home real quick and get it. I promise (crossing my fingers behind my back). I'll be right back in a jiffy."

"I'm sorry sir, no dead people are allowed to leave the morgue by themselves," the coroner says, pointing to a sign on the wall that indeed reads, No dead people are allowed to leave the morgue unattended.

"Maybe you can plead your case to the mortician later when we're done here," he finishes off with while rolling his eyes.

I would of course protest by saying, "Hey, if I were dead or even mostly dead, would I be able to do this?" At this point I would hop down and break out dancing in something that looked like a cross between bad tap dance and someone having a seizure. It would not be pretty and I'm sure if there were parents watching, they would cover their children's eyes and turn away themselves, shaking their heads in disbelief. Some would probably mutter under their breath, "Some people just don't know when they're dead. How sad."

The coroner, not being impressed either, would probably say something like, "Sir, I've seen Zombies that danced way better

I Could Have Had a V8

than that or whatever that was you were trying to do! Now please get back in the drawer, my lunch is getting cold."

Realizing there was no winning against the red tape of bureaucracy, I would finally just admit temporary defeat, climb back in my drawer and start planning my next line of arguments or going over my best escape routes.

Let's just say for fun and keeping in the theme of V8, we are all vegetables. Now that crazy question I have asked others often, comes to mind, "If you were a vegetable, what kind of vegetable would you be?"

If we were vegetables, then God the Father would have been the Big Gardener in the sky who planted and grew us all. He would have sent His Son, Jesus, to become a vegetable like us to redeem us and restore our broken relationship, making a way back to Him because He loved us so much. And as vegetables, as it reads in Genesis, it would also have made great sense for Adam and Eve to be in the "Garden" of Eden. After all, where else would you expect the first two vegetables to be?

And so as vegetables, in need of a Savior . . . we would need a sacrifice. We would need to be covered by the blood of our Great Vegetable Savior (GVS) who died for our sins once and for all. There was no being good enough, no making it on our own. The blood of His only Son is the one and only thing that the Big Gardener (B.G.) would accept. Like the old hymn says, "Are You Washed in the Blood of the Lamb?" That is what would need to happen. And if we were vegetables, the obvious choice for blood that would cover us all would be . . . V8. And when vegetables died that did not accept the gift available to them from B.G. through our GVS, you would hear the words said, "You Could Have Had a V8."

Yes, it's a crazy, crazy story, maybe even lacking meat and substance. But a crazy, crazy story, lacking meat and substance but sprinkled with hidden truth.

Just like the coroner earlier in this story told me I was dead until I proved otherwise, we too are dead without the acceptance of what was done for us on the cross by Jesus taking on and dying for our sins once and for all. Just like our hopeless vegetable friends, we are desperately in need of a Savior. In need of the One that would come, take on and cover our sins with His blood so that He and our Father, could see us as spotlessly clean. Because we are covered by the blood of Jesus, the Father see us through the lens of the sacrifice of His, Son. We are in desperate need of Jesus.

The Bible tells us in Ephesians 2, that we were already dead in our sins. It does not say that we are "mostly dead" but tee-totally dead. Thankfully, that was not the end of the story as far as God was concerned. Because He had this huge, great love for us and He is so merciful, He had to make a way back to Him. He did this by making a way for us to become alive through His Son, Jesus and further making it very clear that there is nothing that we could do to earn it. Nothing could be added or taken away from His perfect plan. It was simply . . . a gift. Not because we deserved it BUT simply because He loved us so much.

Similarly, the Bible also tells us in Romans 6:23 that what we deserve for our sin is simply, death. But it does not stop there, or it would just be a sad, hopeless story. It tells us the bad news but then there is a "but" added to the story. A "but" in the Bible is the coolest thing. It usually represents a you-were-this-but-I-am-doing-this-instead kind of thing. The best description in my mind as far as God is concerned is, "You were hopeless BUT I came and gave you hope." And so it is over and over again with God.

In this instance, the Word is saying, "You deserved death BUT I am going to give you life instead." It's a sweet trade, if you ask me. It is the opportunity for a-beauty-from-ashes transformation. God is holding out the gift of life, free for the asking, made possible through His Son, if we will just accept it. That is the gift.

I Could Have Had a V8

Can you see it? Will you accept it or will you leave it unopened on the table? As always, the choice is up to you.

Daddy, what a great, merciful gift You have offered us all. Not because we deserve it but just because You love us. I am so thankful as I think of this great truth and all the implications it has for me. Like the great hymn, Amazing Grace, says, "I once was lost but now I'm found . . . was blind but now I see." That says it all. Thank You so much for making a way when we had no way on our own. Thank You my Great Deliverer.

Love,

David

Ephesians 2:4-9

But because of his great love for us, God, who is rich in mercy, made us alive with Christ even when we were dead in transgressions—it is by grace you have been saved. And God raised us up with Christ and seated us with him in the heavenly realms in Christ Jesus, in order that in the coming ages he might show the incomparable riches of his grace, expressed in his kindness to us in Christ Jesus. For it is by grace you have been saved, through faith—and this not from yourselves, it is the gift of God—not by works, so that no one can boast.

Romans 6:23

For the wages of sin is death, but the gift of God is eternal life in Christ Jesus our Lord.

A 30-Day Devotional

Have you accepted this free gift that The Big Gardner offers? If so, how has it transformed your life?

Day 7
A Perspective Made of Tears

Today, we have a balmy high of 39 degrees in Boise, Idaho and tomorrow it will be 42!!! I am soooo (four "O's") excited. I know you are wondering what I am all excited about.

If you are some of my friends or family in Pismo Beach, California, you are enjoying a high of 67 degrees today while people in Hampstead, North Carolina are a little chilly at 44 degrees. The good news for Hampstead is that by next Tuesday, they will be back up to 70 degrees while I will still be happy with our Idaho weather which will be 41 degrees by then. You see it's all a matter of perspective and where we have been.

About a month ago, I could be heard in various places complaining about how cold it was when it was a similar temperature as now. Whining then, happy now? What gives? Hormones? Too much chocolate (as if there was such a thing as too much chocolate)? Well, something changed all that.

We have been in an inversion condition, and we have had very, very, cold temperatures for over three weeks in a row. We never warmed up past 20 degrees and our lows for many days were hovering at zero and some days even below. Yes, that is just wrong! That is a far cry from a low of about 30 and a high of 39 . . . a far, far, bone-chilling, ice-forming, finger-freezing, toe-numbing cry.

The snow that we got weeks ago is currently still laying securely on my lawn with no signs of moving anywhere, anytime soon and what was on the side streets is still a nice layer of ice from being driven on. My washer fluid in my car worked yesterday for the first time in weeks, as it warmed up to the freezing mark.

The weather I was complaining about only weeks ago before this cold snap gripped the valley, I am now welcoming with open arms and a kiss of love with my new adjusted perspective. This is the great thing about going through a very, very, cold period during the winter . . . it makes me thankful for and appreciate what I had before.

This very same kind of perspective adjustment happens in other areas of our lives besides the weather. It can be as simple as losing your health for a period of time and then so appreciating wellness when you have it back. It could be losing a job that you had for a long time and maybe did not appreciate until you did not have it anymore and then found that it was much better than what you are finding out there now. It could be a relationship that you took for granted and then all of sudden you found it not there anymore.

Everyone's life is different, and we all walk our own road. I think you get the point and can think of personal things that you can plug in here to fit your own life. The important thing to remember is that where there is loss, there is also the opportunity for gained perspective, added strength, and possible growth in the long run. It's not a guarantee but the opportunity is there. The stinky part in this is that we often have to lose something to make us realize its value. If we are extremely fortunate, we get to learn and not lose something valuable in the process.

A Perspective Made of Tears

In my life, the hardest and most trying times were the VERY ones that have made me the strongest and taught me the most. In that way, there is value to be gained in the good and the bad . . . lessons to be learned . . . perspective to be gained. I will use the hardest time that I have faced in my life as an example.

Anyone who has ever lost a child knows that there is nothing like it. It is wrong in so many ways. There is no way to understand what it is like if it has not happened to you. The person who has lost a child would never want it to happen to anyone to give them that understanding.

Losing my son, Daniel, in a house fire was that hardest time for me. Having to bury my son days before his first birthday did tremendous damage to my soul. I buried a part of my heart that day with my son that I will not get back until I see him again in heaven. There was nothing that could be said to me that would have made it okay for me to be buying Daniel's casket and planning for his funeral, instead of buying him presents and planning for his first birthday. Some things there are no words for.

When we see someone hurting, we are always searching for something comforting to say to them, something to make things better. "He's in a better place" is the one you hear the most. Great for Daniel and very true . . . but that really did not address the deep loss I was feeling and did nothing to fill that huge hole that was left gaping in my heart. But the people trying to help didn't have any way to understand what I was feeling and again, I didn't want them to. And so, I just smiled and said thank you.

In a time like that, I have learned that the best thing you can say to someone may be not much of anything and may be nothing but rather, more listening. And the best thing you can do for them is to be there and walk the long, hard, path beside them so that they are not alone on their journey.

What strength and perspective have I gained from such a loss? Well, right off the bat, I can tell you that things I thought were

A 30-Day Devotional

"BIG DEALS" before I lost my son, Daniel, did not seem to bother me as much anymore. Things that would have caused stress and worry and stole time thinking about them just did not seem that important anymore. That was a major refocus of my perspective.

My strength is now in the fact that I am still kicking after going through that. It was not the end of me as I am very much still here. It was also not the end of hard times but when you compare the hard times of daily life to the loss of your son, they are brought down to proper size. You know that you can face and get through the normal things this life throws at you.

Lastly, I think it gave me understanding into the suffering of others who are facing a similar chapter in their lives. It gave me credentials to share and speak with those people because I have been there. When those people see me still standing here all these years later, loving God and seeing His blessings in my life now, it gives them hope for their future. It gives them hope for a better time down the road when they will be where I am now and maybe helping someone else going through something similar to what they are now. That is a powerful thing and I am thankful for that, even though I am not necessarily thankful for the road that got me to this place.

There is still so much that I don't understand, even all these years later. But that is okay because I love and put my trust in the One that does understand and knows all the reasons for everything I have faced and will face ... the same One that loves me and knit me together in my mother's womb and who now cares for the son that He blessed me with on this earth. And that is enough for now because "now" is not the end. I am waiting for the "then" to come when all things will be made right.

This would be a great place to tie this story up into a nice little package with ribbons and a pretty red bow on top. It would be a nice place, but I would not be doing you a service and I would

A Perspective Made of Tears

not be authentic with you if I did that because . . . there is a catch. (OH NO, not a catch!!!)

What is very, very important to share with you is that I did not understand these things I have been talking about at the time it happened. The hard truth is, my life continued to spiral for many, many years ending with the loss of a marriage which changed many lives forever. We had no idea how hard the grief would hit us and what to do with it when it did. We were not prepared. When it was all over, my marriage was more fallout from an already bad enough situation.

It is very important that you understand that even though I handled many, many things very badly, and in doing so, made things even worse. Even though my life was in a shambles and my trust in God had been shattered into a million pieces, my Father never let me go. He never quit reaching out to me. And over the years, little by little, He kept working in my life and the more I let Him, the more He did. I am only here today . . . I am only who I am and believe how I do, because of God's grace, love, and patience with a broken young man.

The Bible tells us in Romans 8:28 that He will work "all things" for good for those who love Him. That doesn't mean just because you are a Christian, that "all things" that happen to you will be "good things." That is not what it is saying. In my life . . . where the rubber meets the road, it means that God has used and will use "all things," good, bad, and in between to shape and mold me when I let Him. He can teach me, grow me, and mold me from it all. I am proof of that.

Is there something in your life you think is too big or can't be fixed? Well think again. In Psalm 127:1 it tells us that everything we build without God is in vain. With that thought in mind, I would encourage you take on a prayer partner and give your plans over to the Master Builder this very moment.

A 30-Day Devotional

Father, thank You for all the lessons in life … even the very, very, hard ones. Thank You for never giving up on me and making beautiful things in my life.

Love,

David

Revelation 21:3-4

And I heard a loud voice from the throne saying, "Look! God's dwelling place is now among the people, and he will dwell with them. They will be his people, and God himself will be with them and be their God. He will wipe every tear from their eyes. There will be no more death or mourning or crying or pain, for the old order of things has passed away."

Romans 5:1-5

Therefore, since we have been justified through faith, we have peace with God through our Lord Jesus Christ, through whom we have gained access by faith into this grace in which we now stand. And we boast in the hope of the glory of God.

Not only so, but we also glory in our sufferings, because we know that suffering produces perseverance; perseverance, character; and character, hope. And hope does not put us to shame, because God's love has been poured out into our hearts through the Holy Spirit, who has been given to us.

Romans 8:28

And we know that in all things God works for the good of those who love him, who have been called according to his purpose.

A Perspective Made of Tears

Psalm 127:1

Unless the Lord builds the house, the builders labor in vain. Unless the Lord watches over the city, the guards stand watch in vain.

What circumstances in your life have changed your perspective? Have you allowed the Lord to use that situation to make you a better person?

Day 8

Come Hither Heather

On the way to work this morning, I was listening to Adrian Rogers on the radio. He was speaking about the miracle in John 6 where Jesus fed the five thousand with only five small barley loaves of bread and two small fish. He talked about how Jesus asked Phillip, "Where shall we buy bread for these people to eat?" And how He asked Phillip this question only to test him as Jesus already knew that He was going to feed them all and end up with 12 baskets of leftovers.

During this talk, Adrian said the word, "Hither." As soon as he said this word, my mind opened up another window and started playing with that word while I was still listening to the rest of the story. For some reason, I love to say, "Come Hither Heather." Whenever I get the chance to meet a Heather or sometimes when there is no Heather around at all, I just say it, instead of "Hey you, come here!" This morning, my mind was playing with the thought that if I had another baby girl, I could name her, "Hither" and then I could say, "Come Hither," whenever I wanted. And on that run-away-train-of-thought, I could give her the middle name, "Heather" and making me even happier, I could say, "Come Hither Heather," anytime I wanted to!

A 30-Day Devotional

And in case you are wondering, yes, my mind often does this kind of thinking in the middle of other conversations. That is why I often have that silly little grin on my face when you are speaking to me. My mind is actually quite proficient at keeping track of everything pretty well. (I am much too old to have any more kids, so I will never get a chance to use my clever name idea. But now that I have put this great idea in your head, you have the opportunity to make it happen …)

Here is my point: The overall theme to the talk I listened to this morning was about giving everything you have to Jesus. Not just a little of yourself or what you think is fair (50/50, 60/40, 70/30), but rather, all of you—everything you do, everything you say, everything you are and even everything you want to be. Have it all come through Jesus, every single thing. Give him all of your bread and all of your fish, so to speak, and see what He will do with it. To do any less, is limiting what Jesus can do in your life. We cannot receive more, if we refuse to let go of what we are holding on to so tightly. Jesus tells us that if we lose our life for His name's sake, we find it! That's good enough for me!

So what do you think: give all of yourself to Jesus or name your child Hither Heather? The choice is up to you.

Father, Daddy, please teach me to let go. Please teach me to trust. Please teach me that nothing is mine, but rather, everything I have been given is a gift from You. Thank You so much!

Love,

David

John 6:5-6

When Jesus looked up and saw a great crowd coming toward him, he said to Philip, "Where shall we buy bread for these

people to eat?" He asked this only to test him, for he already had in mind what he was going to do.

Matthew 10:39

Whoever finds their life will lose it, and whoever loses their life for my sake will find it.

How can you give more (all) of your life to the Lord? Do you trust Him to take care of you?

Day 9

The Great Conductor

Last night, my wife, Denice, and I watched No Greater Love. I cannot even tell you how many years we have been meaning to go see this production of the life of Jesus. This local church has been putting on this production for the past thirty-four years. We were invited this year by my red-headed daughter, Kelsey, and this year we actually went!

It was great to see Kelsey, her daughter, Amelia, and her boyfriend, Andrew, and the production was fantastic. It is reserved seating and we picked seats online by accident right behind the full orchestra. All the music is played live by the orchestra, which had 30-40 members. There was a percussion area, a xylophones and other things to bonk area, a harp, a stand-up bass, cellos, violins, piano, brass section, drums, an organ, and a few other things I am missing.

It was awesome for me to be so close to them all, even if my view of the stage had to suffer. I am a detail person, so besides what was going on the stage, I was checking out, as best I could, all that I was hearing and what all the different instruments were that were playing all those sweet sounds.

A 30-Day Devotional

I was about six feet from the woman playing harp and I enjoyed watching her skill so closely. I never noticed that harps have pedals . . . and lots of them. I guess I have just been focusing on what fingers were doing in the past. But there is much more going on there, down below the finger movement.

As the music began, I watched all the different instruments playing their own separate parts and working together for the greater good. And though they all were different and playing many various things, when they were blended all together, it was just awesome flowing yumminess to my ears.

Each instrument focused on what they were supposed to play. They did not worry about what all the other instruments were playing. Also, I noticed that all the instruments did not play all the time. Some just had small parts here and there to accent while others had bigger parts that seemed to keep them much busier. But all were important to the whole song and even the production. They all had their own music in front of them with their parts marked out and they followed along until it was time for them to play. Then, when it was their turn, they would play their part with everything they had. Then they would stop and follow along until it was their time again.

One thing I have left out and this is of great importance. EVERYONE watched the conductor. When it was time for a song to begin, the conductor would rise to his feet in front of them all. He would then begin setting and keeping the timing, pointing when a section was to come in or stop and all the while, he was also directing all the singers too. He would mouth the words and give hand signals to the singers keeping them holding a part or stopping them all precisely at his command.

The conductor knew the whole production from start to finish. It did not matter if the individual pieces of the orchestra knew it all, it just mattered that they watched the conductor and came in when they were directed. Without the conductor, things could have and mostly likely would have been a big 30–40-piece mess.

The Great Conductor

It is like that with our lives.

We have a Conductor too. He is the Great Conductor of our lives. He is there, standing in front of us all, keeping the timing of everything, speaking to us, directing us, and encouraging us to do our parts ... to be the Body of Christ. He is orchestrating everything through us, His Body, with His message, to reach a world that is in desperate need of hearing the great story of their redemption.

In His perfect will, we are focused on our parts, not worrying about what other people are doing or even what their parts are. We are following our music and watching the conductor for what HE has for us to do. In His perfect will, we are reflecting a picture of who we love and who gave everything for us.

Out of His perfect will . . . well, it is just the opposite in every way and much like an orchestra that is not watching or listening to their wise conductor. It is in short . . . a mess.

WE, you and me, are a beautiful illustration of the Body of Christ, each doing our different things, playing different parts, and working together for the greater good. Oh yes, we may not be so beautiful and great at the "togetherness and oneness thing" now . . . but one day when Jesus has perfected us . . . watch out.

Great Conductor, I am thankful and honored to be a part of Your big, beautiful plan. Please help me to play my parts skillfully. Please help me to keep my focus on You and all that You have for me in this life. Help me to be content with what You have for me and not to worry about what You have for others. Please keep me and guide me so that I can become skillful and be something useful in Your great production.

Love,

David

A 30-Day Devotional

Romans 12:4-8

For just as each of us has one body with many members, and these members do not all have the same function, so in Christ we, though many, form one body, and each member belongs to all the others. We have different gifts, according to the grace given to each of us. If your gift is prophesying, then prophesy in accordance with your faith; if it is serving, then serve; if it is teaching, then teach; if it is to encourage, then give encouragement; if it is giving, then give generously; if it is to lead, do it diligently; if it is to show mercy, do it cheerfully.

Hebrews 12:1-5

Therefore, since we are surrounded by such a great cloud of witnesses, let us throw off everything that hinders and the sin that so easily entangles. And let us run with perseverance the race marked out for us, fixing our eyes on Jesus, the pioneer and perfecter of faith. For the joy set before him he endured the cross, scorning its shame, and sat down at the right hand of the throne of God. Consider him who endured such opposition from sinners, so that you will not grow weary and lose heart.

What has the Great Conductor given you to play? How can you focus more on what is yours and not get distracted by what others are doing?

Day 10

A Batty Perspective

My wife, Denice, daughter, Kendra, and I were the first to arrive at camp. We had a slew of people from our Alpha group that meets at our church coming up and we expected them all in the next few hours. The ride up to Cascade, Idaho, had been uneventful, but as we continued to the YWAM camp, which is above Cascade near Warm Lake, the color outside the car began to turn much whiter.

First it was patches of land on each side of the road, then the trees, and soon bits of the road we were driving on would be covered in the white stuff. This slowed us down a little, but we were still making good time. When we hit the peak and started to come down the backside, everything had now changed to the color white, including our faces going around some of the corners. It was slow going from that point on. We were glad when we finally pulled into the camp and parked by the lodge that we had completed the drive before the sun went down.

I went inside to check on the cabin sleeping arrangements while the girls waited in the car and my wife, who had been driving, tried to pry her white knuckles from the steering wheel. This was my third time visiting this camp and I had always stayed in the bigger cabins, each big enough to sleep at least a dozen people if needed. Chris, one of the directors, told me about some smaller cabins off to the left of the lodge that I was not familiar with. But because I was familiar with the places I had stayed at before, I just chose to stay where I had always stayed the previous times, sticking to what I knew. This is often not the best choice in life and it was not the best choice here either as it would turn out.

These big cabins also did not have a bathroom, so you had to walk about 50 yards to do your business. That required planning ahead and being ready at all times to wrestle a bear or mountain lion in the white stuff on the way to or back from the bathroom.

We were there two hours before the next couple, Terry and Lynn, arrived. Terry checked out those cabins that I had passed on without even looking at. Because of his willingness to look, he scored a smaller cabin with a single room on one side including a bathroom, a living room in the middle, and then another room without a bathroom on the other side. I too could have had this place had I taken a chance to go where I had not been before.

My wife was less than pleased with our spacious cabin when she saw what we could have had behind door number one. But in my defense, in my cabin choice, you could set your alarm for every hour on the hour, switch to a new bed each time the alarm went off and never be in the same bed twice. I know, cool right? There is something to be said about that. (There was surely something to be said about that alright, but it was not a very nice "something" for sure.)

While I was at the big cabin, one of the gals at the YWAM camp took my wife on a tour of what was left of the smaller cabins behind door number two and three. It was quickly decided, much to my dismay, that we were moving out of the spacious bed laden cabin, into a measly two bed, much smaller but closer to everything cabin. And though it did not have its own bathroom, the main bathrooms were much closer.

A Batty Perspective

So, with my imaginary tail between my legs, I gathered up all our things, put them back in the RAV4, drove it back behind the lodge and unloaded it all again into the unoccupied cabin . . . or so I thought. (Bum . . . bum . . . bum—scary music plays.)

I must admit that it actually WAS nice to be so centrally located. (But I would never admit that out loud). At first, we had some heating issues in our cozy little cabin, but that was resolved quickly with another heater put into the room. That night, I tucked my guitar and Denice's bass into the extra bed, covered them up with a nice blanket, making sure the neck of my guitar was comfortably on the pillow. Then Denice and I hit the hay in the other bed and got a good night's rest without incident (though I did have a dream about a puppy licking my face which made me giggle in my sleep).

After the morning classes, we both retreated to the cabin until lunch. I was sitting on our bed and Denice was in front of me, sitting in a stuffed chair facing me. The instrument's bed was to my left and the door was in Denice's direct sight but behind me, to my right. With the room clearly drawn in your mind, here is what happened next.

On the instrument's bed, I heard something flop. I was looking at some PowerPoint slides and looked up but did not see anything. I asked Denice, "Did you just throw something onto the bed? I heard something flop onto it."

She said, "No and don't try to scare me." I told her I wasn't trying to scare her but thought I had heard something like a book being thrown onto the bed. Denice went back to her book and I went back to my PowerPoint.

In my peripheral vision, I saw something take off from the bed and land in the middle of the floor between Denice and me. As I looked to see what had landed and realized what it was, Denice also looked and thought she saw a pine cone between us. Before I could say anything, she stuck her foot out to push it with the tip of her shoe and the pine cone took flight. It was at this point that she also knew she had just kicked a bat in the butt!

There was lots of high-pitched screaming and yelling and sounds like a little girl crying. Denice also made a few sounds of her own, but I was too involved in my own panic to notice. When the bat took flight after being kicked in the butt by Denice, we both yelled. I then rolled backward onto the bed while kicking my legs in the air and cried for my momma, while she pulled her feet up into the chair and transformed into the shape of a screaming pine cone.

After an unknown amount of time, and the panic had passed, I saw that the bat had landed by the broom to the left of the front door and then crawled behind it. I told Denice that I was going to open the front door and for her to leave quickly when I did. Part of me just wanted to run out the door and keep running until my direction was changed by bouncing off a tree, building, bear or mountain lion. But this was no time to be a coward. It was a time to throw down and be a man. It was going to be man against bat . . . bat against man . . . may the better mammal win. Yes, it was mano a mano. (Or would that be mano a bato?) Whatever it was, it was on!

After Denice was safely out of the cabin, I opened the door wide and moved the broom giving the bat a chance to use the chicken exit if he was not up to a battle. But this was no cowardly bat and as soon as the broom was moved, he quickly lunged forward trying to take out my jugular for the quick win. Of course, I anticipated this move from all my years of "hand to bat" combat classes and as he took flight, my ninja, catlike reflexes kicked in and I began to sweep. And this was no gingerly, "Hey, look at me, I'm sweeping a dust bunny," kind of sweeping I was doing. I swept like no one has ever swept before and may never sweep again.

When the dust settled, the almost wolf-sized bat had been swept outside and flew, red-faced, into the nearby trees in defeat. Yes,

A Batty Perspective

my broom and I had once again faced a very close "brush" with death. I had "whisked" my very life in this fight to the death or at least to the hang nail. And when it was all over and I had been carried around the camp on the shoulders of the cheering crowd, I carved yet another notch into my broom handle.

One would think this was the end of the story. But "one" would be wrong. You see, I got to thinking about my amazing feat of bravery and remarkably humble attitude and wondered if maybe there was another viewpoint to this story that I was missing. Then it occurred to me … what was the bat thinking? Did he have anything to add to this story? Would his opinion change anything? Here are my thoughts on that.

> I had moved into a very nice cabin with two bedrooms that had been unoccupied for some time. I hate rooming with those pesky humans, because they can't seem to go without opening the door 100 times a day. Then last Friday, everything changed. From my view from under bed, I saw four legs come in and some high-pitched voices talking back and forth and then they were gone. I was happy about that. I was going to peek out and see who they were, but they left before I could get my head out.
>
> A while later, I saw two legs come in but these looked like sad, dejected legs and there was an imaginary tail hanging between these legs. There were some grumbling sounds coming from this one also as he tossed things everywhere in my place. I was not happy, but since I had not signed an official lease and was "squatting," I decided to stay put and see what happened before I made a stink.
>
> That night was pretty uneventful. Four legs come back later that night and after something was put in my bed without even asking and a blanket given to it, the four legs laid down in their bed and went to sleep. I crawled out a few times and licked the bigger two legs' face while he was sleeping because it would make him giggle and I got a kick out of it.

A 30-Day Devotional

(For those of you going ew! I made the bat licking and giggle part up just for fun.) Then I went back under the bed and attended to my bat business and hoped these guys would be moving out soon.

The next morning, they did leave but they didn't take their stuff with them so I figured they'd be back. A little before lunch, the four legs came through the door again. The bigger two legs went and sat on one bed while the smaller two legs went and sat in the chair in the middle of the room.

Well, I had just about enough and decided to go have a little chat with these four legs and let them know, "I was here first." If that didn't work, I would just do some of my bat tricks which usually worked pretty well at clearing places out.

I climbed up between the wall and bed and plopped myself on the second bed. At this point, I saw the bigger two legs look over at me but for some reason he did not see me. He said something to the smaller two legs and then they both went back to what they were doing. I was thinking, "Hello, Bat here!" But it was no use, they were not seeing it. So I did a little flying maneuver and landed on the floor in between them both. This seem to get the bigger two legs attention as he looked right at me and his eyes got bigger and started to dilate. "Finally," I thought. Just about then something goosed me firmly right on my keister. I was like, "Whoa Nelly" and before I knew what happened, I instinctively took flight.

All of a sudden there was a tremendous amount of high-pitched screaming and yelling and sounds like a little girl crying. Even the smaller two legs made a little noise. Bigger two legs had rolled backward onto the bed and appeared to be riding an imaginary bicycle in the air, while the smaller two legs had curled up into some kind of ball in the chair and there was now a high pitch noise coming from her that was hurting my ears, to tell you the truth. I was not sure what all the ruckus was about, so I decided it might be safer

A Batty Perspective

for me to find a place to hide myself, until I found out. So I went and hid behind the broom in the corner of the room.

The next thing I knew it got much brighter but I was still behind the broom so it was bearable. There was some talking back and forth and then I think I saw the smaller two legs run out the door while flailing her arms like a chicken. It was a funny sight for sure and I chuckled to myself. I was waiting for bigger two legs to follow suit, but that didn't happen. Instead, all of a sudden, the broom was pulled out of the way and I was hit by a blinding bright light. I tried to fly away from the light and back under my bed but I kept hitting this moving wall. Over and over and over again it continued to whack me. It whacked me until all of a sudden I found myself lying outside in the snow. I got up quickly because the snow was very cold on my little bat belly and flew off to some nearby trees to sort out what had just happened to me.

So, two very different stories, right? But do you know what the most interesting thing is to me? Both stories are as true as the other from their separate perspectives. If you heard the four legs version of the story, that is what you would believe and if you heard the Bat's version of the story, you would believe that instead. The "real" story is somewhere in between the two. The only way to get the big picture would be to hear both sides of the story.

It is not hard to see where I am going with this. Life works like this, doesn't it? Is not perspective the most important thing in understanding a situation and working through a problem and really solving an issue? Not just one perspective either or you likely are not seeing the whole picture, but as many perspectives as you can get from people who are involved in that situation. Without all of the information, how can you really solve anything? Most times I find that after hearing the entire story, the solution lies somewhere in the middle of all you have heard. Something to think seriously about when life comes at you hard and swift and relationships lay in the balance.

A 30-Day Devotional

In my experience, so many problems in my life have boiled down to a misunderstanding of a situation. Sometimes I have been able to resolve a situation by talking through the different viewpoints and had my understanding grow as things were talked through. But then there are some situations in my life that have remained unresolved because one person cannot solve a problem on their own. Both sides have to be willing or it is just the "Bat's" vs. "Four Legs'" version kind of thing. But even in those situations, we still need to do all that we can do from OUR side to fix a problem. My wife refers to it as, "Keeping your side of the street clean." I like that analogy.

We are to interact with people with love, even with ones that drive us a little batty. James tells us that we need to be quick to listen, slow to speak, and slow to anger. What great advice that is for sure. I tend to be slow to listen and quick to speak and get angry. That doesn't work so well. Because of our inadequacies as humans, I think the most important thing we need to be able to do is forgive, not just for the other people but for ourselves. Often we can forgive others much more easily than we can forgive ourselves. I don't know what is up with that. Maybe it is because we know ourselves so well. One thing is for sure, we will all make mistakes and without forgiveness, we have no hope at all.

Father, how often I find myself and my attitudes in direct opposition to what I read in Your Word. How many times will I battle with the same issues over and over in this life? How many times will I come to You, sorry and broken, and have You forgive and start me over clean? Only You know the day and the hour and the minute that You will sweep me into ultimate freedom in You. I look forward to every victory in You, Father. Thanks so much for Your patience and the great love You have for me. (Oh, and Bat . . . I forgive you. Please forgive me also . . . Signed, Two Legs).

Love,

David

A Batty Perspective

James 1:19-20

My dear brothers and sisters, take note of this: Everyone should be quick to listen, slow to speak and slow to become angry, because human anger does not produce the righteousness that God desires.

Ephesians 4:31-32

Get rid of all bitterness, rage and anger, brawling and slander, along with every form of malice. Be kind and compassionate to one another, forgiving each other, just as in Christ God forgave you.

Matthew 6:14-15

For if you forgive other people when they sin against you, your heavenly Father will also forgive you. But if you do not forgive others their sins, your Father will not forgive your sins.

Is there a person who you need to forgive because of a hard situation? What might their perspective of the situation be? How would your life change if you extended forgiveness?

Day 11
One Leg In, One Leg Out

I am a one leg in, one leg out . . . kind of guy. (OLIOLO for you acronym lovers like myself.) I am not really sure when it all started or if I just came out of the womb with this natural propensity. If so, I'm sure being wrapped like a burrito in the hospital nursery drove me plum crazy. I am also pretty sure that if there was a way to pop my leg out of my burrito wrap, I did it—much to the frustration of the nursery nurses.

Now there are some places where you should not have one leg in and one leg out for sure. Trains, planes, and automobiles are the first to come to mind when I process this thought. In these three examples, you are usually only allowed to make that mistake once. From that point on, you normally don't have a leg to stand on. Riding a horse would be another that could spur a little trouble or saddle you with a situation. Wearing your pants OLIOLO at work would probably also not be recommended and could cause quite a commotion. This could lead to you either getting fired or starting a new, hip, right on, out-of-sight fashion trend. Stranger things have happened. Anything would be better than the baggy pants barely hanging on your hip thingy. Just sayin'.

A 30-Day Devotional

But then there is an ordained time and place for the OLIOLO mode of operation. Right off the bat, the most obvious is while doing the Hokey Pokey!!! It actually could be and should be the theme song to OLIOLO!

During that song, it is perfectly acceptable to put your right leg in, and then put your right leg out. And just when you thought it could not get any better, you get to put it right back in again which leads to the greatest way to highlight the whole wonderful celebration where you are then allowed to … shake it all about. I know, I know. Exciting!!! Only then, can you do the Hokey Pokey and commence to TURN YOURSELF AROUND! Why you ask? Well simply, because "that's what it's all about!" I love America!!!

How wonderful and marvelous this celebration is for an OLIOLO kind of guy. It is hard to get . . . well . . . dare I say it? Okay, I will. It is hard to get a leg up on that kind of celebration!

It seems to me that there is a time and a place for most everything in this life. (Play the song "Turn! Turn! Turn!" by the Byrds in your head now.) So far, I have been writing about a lot of things and really have only touched on what the main focus of this story is about, my sleeping style preference. I know what you are thinking. Isn't it pretty close to, "Why didn't you tell me this right off in the first paragraph so I could be long gone by now?" Anyway, I will focus on that now.

I love to sleep with one leg in and one leg out. More correctly, my whole body in but with one leg, usually my right one, sticking out from under the covers to various degrees during the night. I do this because I sleep, temperature wise, on the hot side. Putting one leg out at different times and lengths is a way for me to cool down and regulate my temperature. Sometimes I will resort to both legs in but two feet out (BLIBTFO) but that is not the norm and should only be attempted by a professional for sure. Because of that, I will not even mention it.

One Leg In, One Leg Out

What is the point of all this? Why is this important in the slightest? Well, maybe it isn't. Maybe I was just trying to show you that I could write over a page and a half on something that was really pretty dull all in itself and you would read it anyway. (Loud murmuring heard in the crowd.) Or maybe, just maybe, I can pull something of value out of my hat.

Last week, I woke up in the middle of the night a little overheated and popped my leg out to begin cool down. I was a little restless and was having a hard time going back to sleep. In my head, I began to pray for people who came to mind. While I was doing this, the thought of how I liked to put my leg out to regulate my temperature was a good thing but when it came to my commitment to God, it was not okay at all. Thinking more on this, I thought how we are instructed and encouraged in the Word of God to be "all in" when it comes to our commitment to Him.

It was apparent to me that I, at least (but probably all of us), struggle to stay "all in" at times. It seems during times of doubt, hard times, and struggles, we have arms and legs and perhaps our whole body out from the "covers" or "covering" of God. Do we "really" trust God in "all" things or just in the things we pick and choose and only when things are going well? When we doubt in the hard times, do we run to other things and/or other ways—like maybe a "Plan B?" If we have a "Plan B," we are certainly not "all in." In my life, I have probably been guilty of having a whole alphabet "B-Z Plan" when all I should have is "Plan A" or "God's Plan."

The Bible is clear that God wants to have an "all in" kind of relationship with us. He wants us to always be on fire for Him and powered in our whole lives by His Holy Spirit, not just on Sunday and every other Thursday except on a leap year. He wants "all things" to come through our commitment to Jesus instead of us having "all these things" and then Jesus too when we have time. He doesn't want to be a part of our life; He wants to be all our life—everything—all of it—sold out to Him. He wants all of us, the good, bad, and everything in between—the whole kit and caboodle. It's a beauty for ashes kind of deal for Him, there is no doubt. But that's what He asks, for us to bring Him our all.

If you want a close relationship with your wife/husband, girlfriend/boyfriend, you have to pursue it and you have to work at it. It does not just happen, it is hard, hard work and if you stop, the relationship will suffer. It is only as good and as strong as your commitment to that relationship. The exact same thing applies to our relationship with God.

He is there waiting for us to find all that He has for us. But so often we are pursuing so many things that we have little or no time to find anything in Him, much less, an abundant life. And then we wonder what is wrong and why God seems so far away. The problem is us—the problem is we are not "all in."

If we really want to know God, we must give Him everything: our hopes, our dreams, our disappointments, our possessions, our talents, our loved ones—everything. None of it really belongs to us anyway. I know that is a hard thought, but it is a true thought. All we have, had, and will have, all we are, have been, will ever be—it all belongs to God anyway. He is our Creator and the Creator of all the good things that He made for us. By letting go of all these things, we gain God and can make Him the center of our lives. The Bible concept is that by losing our lives, we save it. That is because we find God when we give it all back to the One that owns it all anyway.

Our job is not to let anything get in the way of our relationship with God. And when we find something that is in the way, we must be willing to let God take it away. We should strive to worship God with all our heart, soul, mind, and strength and live all of our life in Him and through Him. If we can do this, I believe that God will bring all the things we really need to us. We need

One Leg In, One Leg Out

to sacrifice all of our "Plan Bs" and get our commitment legs "all in" and back fully under the cover of the One that loves us the most and knows us the best.

Daddy, the more I grow and the more I seek to know You, the more I see how far I have to go. I have a lot of work to do in my life and I want to be "all in" with You for that reconstruction. Crumble all the things I hold on to in this life that are not rooted in You and keep me from moving closer to You. Open my eyes to things I need to see and things I need to change in my life, even if it is painful. Then give me the strength in You, to walk away to freedom. I thank You in advance and love You, Great Lover of My Soul.

Love,

David

Revelation 3:15-16

I know your deeds, that you are neither cold nor hot. I wish you were either one or the other! So, because you are lukewarm—neither hot nor cold—I am about to spit you out of my mouth.

Mark 8:34-36

Then he called the crowd to him along with his disciples and said: "Whoever wants to be my disciple must deny themselves and take up their cross and follow me. For whoever wants to save their life will lose it, but whoever loses their life for me and for the gospel will save it. What good is it for someone to gain the whole world, yet forfeit their soul?"

A 30-Day Devotional

Jeremiah 29:11-13

"For I know the plans I have for you," declares the Lord, "plans to prosper you and not to harm you, plans to give you hope and a future. Then you will call on me and come and pray to me, and I will listen to you. You will seek me and find me when you seek me with all your heart."

Do you feel that you are "all in" with Jesus? If not, what areas of your life do you need to give to Him? How will your life be different when you do?

Day 12
A Grizzly Business Deal

Last night, in the black of night, I woke up with a thought on my mind. You would think it would be a very important thought if my mind woke me up in the middle of the night to share it with me. And indeed, it was.

As I laid there, this is the thought that clearly came into focus. "If I were to open a sushi restaurant, would I want to have a grizzly bear as my partner?"

I know, I know, very, very deep. I smiled to myself. Since it was dark, I have no way of knowing for sure if my mouth was co-operating or still sleeping. I figured this thought was here for a reason so I methodically contemplated the pros and cons of such a business adventure.

The first thing that came to my mind was the vast experience the grizzly bear had with sushi. Sure, sure, not quite in the same

A 30-Day Devotional

form that people are used to eating it in but there was no doubt that grizzly bears had been eating raw fish their whole lives. As I write this, visions of grizzly bears standing in a river catching salmon swimming upstream are playing in my head. Did you see that one jump and how that grizzly bear caught him in midair? Wowee, if we could incorporate that into the restaurant, think of how that would draw the people in.

Of course, there are logistics associated with that. The restaurant would need to be built over a river with various fish swimming upstream for my bear and fish catching extravaganza. I guess it would also be possible to build an artificial river through the restaurant with a glass bottom of course. Then when people would order their sushi, employees eagerly waiting and staged in the backroom, would grab your fish from a well-stocked aquarium, put them in the river and send them swimming upstream for the grizzly bear to catch in midair. Then the grizzly would politely hand the freshly caught fish (FCF) to the chef who would prepare them to your exact order. Better yet, if I could train the grizzly bear to prepare the order, it would be even faster. He could wear a really cute high white chef hat and matching white chef outfit. Wow, who would not love to see all that? The lines would be out the door for sure.

There is no doubt that the vast experience with raw fish would be a huge asset to consider when going into business with a grizzly bear. They are also very strong and could probably work long hours and would be great at loading and unloading heavy freight delivered to the restaurant. I think you would want to work them as much as possible before winter because their inclination to hibernation (ITH) may become an issue and would be something to work out clearly in their contract. With that thought, I guess we should consider the possible downsides too.

First off, the main downside is that they are grizzly bears and that can make them a little unpredictable. I'm sure they didn't just get that name "grizzly" for no reason in particular. Some

A Grizzly Business Deal

got the name black bears and some brown bears, but they were given "grizzly" before their bear name. We should not forget that as it may mean something pretty important. In being a bear and being unpredictable, you could probably not reason with them like you could with people. But then again, I have met many people that I could not really reason with either so I really can't hold that against them.

Second, grizzly bears are also pretty hairy so hair might occasionally get into the food. A simple hair and beard net would not fix this problem I'm afraid and getting them to wax all of the other areas would be impossible.

But the biggest problem I see is that maybe once the fish had been put in the artificial river from the backroom and had swum upstream and been caught in midair, maybe the bear would not want to hand the freshly caught fish (FCF) over politely to the chef to be prepared for someone else. Maybe—just maybe—he would want to keep it for himself. And if he did, I'm not sure that arguing with him at that point would work out well. Hand it over. Hand it over this instant! Threatening to put him on probation or docking his pay would probably not mean much to him either. Putting up a sign that read, "Bears are not allowed to eat fish while they are on the clock" would probably be a nice gesture but since grizzly bears or bears in general don't read, it would probably still not help.

Frankly, I think that if the grizzly bear wanted to eat the fish that he caught, he would get to eat the fish. And if he wanted to eat the next fish and next one and the next one . . . no one is probably going to say much to him. This scenario could really slow things down and I don't think the customers would be very happy. Again, I don't think they would say a whole lot directly to the grizzly bear because they know that the grizzly bear may just put the fish down and eat the complaining people instead!!! And eating customers in any country is still very much frowned upon. But it might keep them from coming back the next time.

And of course, that could have a "bearing" on the success of the business. (What? I have been holding back "bear" puns this whole time. You should "paws" and instead be proud of me that I have only let one—I mean two—slip out.)

In considering all the pros and cons from above, my conclusion—sad as it may be—is that I do not think that grizzly bears and people are compatible when it comes to opening a sushi restaurant. Maybe Panda bears are easier to work with as Panda Express does seem to be a success.

Life can work very much like this. "Really?" you ask. And to that I would say, "Well yes, yes it does!"

First off, life can certainly be a little "grizzly." (Buzz! . . . that's three bear puns, mister!) And at times, it can seem like it is "unbearable." (Buzz! . . . that's it, 10 minutes in the pun penalty box—the PPB.) And at times, it just seems like I had to "claw" my way through the day, crying out to my Heavenly "PAW PAW" for help just to make it through. (What, are you serious? Now a double pun?) And it would take everything I could do not to just "cave" in and give up. (Heavy sigh of defeat.)

Okay, now that I have finally got those pesky pun thoughts out of my head, I can continue on the final "bearing" for this story.

The Word of God tells us that we should be careful of the company we keep. In the example above, we would not want to go into business with someone that did not have the same business and moral standards as we did, much less, someone who could eat us if we made them mad. Linking our lives with likeminded people should go for all our important relationships, from our close friends to our boy/girlfriends and especially who we marry.

Successful people in all categories are usually surrounded by likeminded successful and supportive people. If you want to be married 50 years and beyond, you should surround yourselves

A Grizzly Business Deal

with likeminded people and get to know couples that have obtained just that. To take advice to someone who has been married seven times would be as foolish as going into the restaurant business with a grizzly bear.

For anything you want to do and be successful at, whether it be personal, relational, business, etc., linking yourself with likeminded thinkers is wise. There is strength and support in numbers. We are stronger together. Linking with the people that have already made it to where you want to go is also wise. A mentor in your life is a great gift.

In saying all this, I am not saying we are not to have anything to do with people that think differently than we do. I have all kinds of friends, many that think very, very differently than I do. I have respectful relationships with those people. But my closest friends, the ones that I choose to let in and trust to speak into my life, are people that are likeminded and have similar goals and lifestyles. We should all have a core of people in our lives like this. Small church home groups are great for this kind of connection.

In closing, consider who you are allowing to speak into your lives. Should all of the people who come to mind be there? Which of them have your best interest? Are they likeminded? Are they heading in the same direction that you are?

Boundaries are important and we have freewill, but we are responsible for what and who we choose. Ask God to help you draw the boundaries that He wants for you. Ask Him to show you by His Holy Spirit where they are now and where they should be. Then I encourage you to begin the journey to make that change.

Daddy, thanks for waking me up last night and asking me such a crazy question to make me think. I love how You interact with me and how You allow me to learn what You are saying to me. Please help me to choose wisely who I allow to speak into my life. Show me clearly who You put in my path and who you are clearing from my roads. Give me the strength, will, and determination to take the steps that will lead me to where You want me to be. Thank You in advance Great Lover of my soul.

Love,

David

1 Corinthians 15:33

Do not be misled: "Bad company corrupts good character."

2 Corinthians 6:14-15

Do not be yoked together with unbelievers. For what do righteousness and wickedness have in common? Or what fellowship can light have with darkness? What harmony is there between Christ and Belial? Or what does a believer have in common with an unbeliever?

What people do you have in your life that are likeminded and encouraging? In what areas of your life do you need a mentor who has been successful in that area?

Day 13

Floppy Bags

Hello, my name is David Wood and I used to have floppy bags. Sometimes, I just think it is best to come right out and put it all on the table right up front. Then the elephant in the room is out in the open and you can only move forward from that point on. The ice has been broken and progress can now be made.

When I was younger, I don't think I ever had any bags to even worry about. But now here I was at 52 years old, noticing that I indeed had floppy bags. It all started about a year ago. If I can be vulnerable with you, it was really annoying and to be honest, a little embarrassing at times. I tried securing them in place when it first started happening and that was somewhat better. But then sometimes when I was not paying attention, my top would open up if the wind got too hard and blew just right and expose my stuff to the entire world, sometimes without me even knowing about it.

I would just be going along, minding my business and then something would bump me in the back. I would look back to see my top opening and closing and things flapping in the wind and sometimes some of my stuff would start to hang out. I would

A 30-Day Devotional

have to hold my top down until I could come to a stop and clip and snap it back in place. This got old very fast.

Of course, you know I am talking about the saddle bags on my motorcycle. If not, I'm sure you just let out a big sigh of relief.

The problem with my motorcycle was created by the original owner. Instead of getting the motorcycle equipped with a touring package that included a windshield, passenger back rest and side bags, they had opted to save $1000 and buy all aftermarket equipment. The problem was, the bags were inferior to the ones that would have come with the motorcycle. The rest was a pretty good imitation but still not the original equipment designed by the manufacturer and thus, not authentic.

The bags were the worst of the three pieces. They were a little too long and hung down slightly farther on the left side to keep the right side slightly higher to avoid touching the exhaust pipe and melting that bag.

It was my last experience on the freeway going about 70 mph that was the final straw (if motorcycles on a freeway have such a thing). After getting bumped in the back, I notice my left bag had come completely open and was flapping all over and some of my cold gear was trying to crawl out and make an escape. I had to drive a couple miles on the freeway with my left hand holding the bag closed and my right hand on the gas. This is not my choice of how I would like to ride on the freeway on my motorcycle! I knew something had to change.

That change ended up with me looking for a replacement for my floppy bags. I ran across an ad on Craigslist for an original windshield, passenger back rest and, bags. I got a screaming deal and picked it all up for $200.

The original bags had a frame that bolted right to the side of the motorcycle and then the bags bolted on to the frame. When installed, "as was intended by the manufacturer," they were solid

Floppy Bags

and secure. In fact, I just may have the most stable bags in town or possibly in the greater northwest. Each piece also had the official "Boulevard" logo, insuring these were in fact, authentic and made specifically for this motorcycle. And with that one switch in place, David Wood had shed his floppy bags and things would never be the same.

Floppy is often not a good thing. If you are known as a flip-flopper that is not a good thing. If you write a Broadway play and the review on the show says it was a flop, that's not good either. If you jump off a diving board and attempt to do a flip but you don't quite get the whole revolution in and land on your belly, that is known as a belly flop and is not generally considered a success.

All this flip-flop talk reminds me of a verse in James that talks about doubt being like a wave of the sea that is blown and tossed around by the wind. And further, if we are like that, not to expect anything from God because we are unstable.

Unstable? Wow, harsh! And don't expect anything from God? Yikes! That sounds like a big deal and indeed, it is. So why is that? Well, this is what I think.

God does not want us to be lukewarm. The Word tells us that He wants us to be hot or cold and if we are in the middle that we are in danger of being spit out of His mouth. God wants to be our source from which everything else flows, not just one of the things we go to when it is convenient or something is wrong and we need help. We are clearly told to seek the Kingdom of God first before anything else. The problem comes because we seek many, many other things and then, every now and then, try to fit the Kingdom of God in somewhere—if we don't run out of time. "Okay, God, I've got three minutes before I have to run to my yoga class. I would catch some time with you when I get home, but I have to watch the season finale of Law and Order: SVU. So I guess this is OUR time. Give me everything You've got for me. I'm all ears . . . Oops, sorry, gotta take this call."

God wants us to know what we believe and to stand firm in that truth. But how can we know what we believe and what God's truth is if we don't spend any time learning about it? He does not want us to kind of believe and then flop when the winds blow, throwing our baggage all over the freeway. He wants us to have and know everything we need, to stand firm and solid and weather the fiercest storm.

God is our Original Manufacturer and He wants to be our exclusive source for everything we need along this ride we call life. Only He has everything that we really and truly need. But often we don't like what that looks like. Just like with my motorcycle, we trade the original equipment for a cheap substitute that looks like a better deal and seems like it will not cost us as much. And just like my floppy bags, in time, we see that all we believed was just a cheap imitation, a big fat lie even, and does not give us what we really need and costs us greatly in retrospect. All the while, there stands our loving Father watching and waiting.

I think God is asking us to take inventory and to remove all the things we have put on "aftermarket," if you will. You know what I am talking about, all the things that we have picked up along the way for added security and/or comfort but that take our attention and/or focus off and away from our One and only true hope. God wants us to be authentic and it is hard to be authentic if we have all this aftermarket floppy baggage in the way. God is not interested in us just "looking good," He actually wants to help us work on "becoming good." And only because of God, there is hope.

If we will let Him, He will help us remove all the things that hinder, slow, and weigh us down in this life. He will strip it all away and start us clean. Then He will install solid truth that was designed specifically for us by our Great Manufacturer. You will also notice that everything He installs will have the logo of the Holy Spirit, the same One that sealed our salvation in the blood of Jesus. This truth is solid and immovable and can withstand

Floppy Bags

any storm this life throws at us . . . if we will just leave it on and stand in it.

What do you say . . . are you tired of flopping? Are you ready for the real thing?

My Father, I am in constant need of an overhaul and redesign. And though I know I need all this work, I am confident that by Your grace, You are hard at work on me and I am grateful to You, my Great Manufacturer. Thank You so much for never giving up on me. Thank You for seeing me as Your finished product instead of as how I see me, with all my flaws and imperfections. As always, I stand amazed at the love You have for me and for us all.

Love . . . Your work in progress,

David

James 1:5-8

If any of you lacks wisdom, you should ask God, who gives generously to all without finding fault, and it will be given to you. But when you ask, you must believe and not doubt, because the one who doubts is like a wave of the sea, blown and tossed by the wind. That person should not expect to receive anything from the Lord. Such a person is double-minded and unstable in all they do.

Matthew 6:33

But seek first his kingdom and his righteousness, and all these things will be given to you as well.

A 30-Day Devotional

Colossians 3:12

Therefore, as God's chosen people, holy and dearly loved, clothe yourselves with compassion, kindness, humility, gentleness and patience.

Ephesians 4:22-24

You were taught, with regard to your former way of life, to put off your old self, which is being corrupted by its deceitful desires; to be made new in the attitude of your minds; and to put on the new self, created to be like God in true righteousness and holiness.

Hebrews 12:1-2

Therefore, since we are surrounded by such a great cloud of witnesses, let us throw off everything that hinders and the sin that so easily entangles. And let us run with perseverance the race marked out for us, fixing our eyes on Jesus, the pioneer and perfecter of faith. For the joy set before him he endured the cross, scorning its shame, and sat down at the right hand of the throne of God.

What "aftermarket" or imitation product have you believed in your life? Ask the Holy Spirit to show you and replace it with God's truth.

Day 14
Getting in the Groove

In the mornings when I get to work, I am pretty predictable and yesterday was no different. As usual, I got my water bottle and Styrofoam coffee cup that I was re-using and took off for the break room to refill them both.

Everything went as planned with my coffee.

Now Micron has never and will never be accused of having the best coffee. There is no doubt of that. It is not robust to say the least and you will never find Juan Valdez sitting there with his donkey handing you your first, fresh, piping hot cup of joe through the window like in the commercial. But that doesn't happen often at home either so my expectation may be set a little too high.

What you will find are many big containers containing something that does resemble coffee and has the best attribute of all . . . it is free. And nearby are the dispensers for sugar, fake sugar, and powdered cream so you can doctor it up and make it tolerable to the palate. Again, being free carries a lot of weight here. But if you like, you CAN buy from the coffee shop we have on site in the cafeteria or get a foo-foo coffee from the vending machine. But in my book, free wins here hands down. You might say I like to count my beans. You may filter that statement however you like.

After filling my cup with the so-called, "coffee," I moved on to the ice and water dispenser. The ice and water mix is crucial and must be at exactly the right ratio. One or two percent in one direction or the other can wreak havoc on the rest of the day. Okay, not really, I was just attempting to fill a couple more lines to make this slightly more interesting than it already is not. Anyway, when I went to screw on the lid so I could begin my journey back to my desk, something went awry.

My lid is threaded and has grooves in it that when lined up, screw it tightly to the top of the container, sealing it against leaks. But though I had screwed it on, it was just a little off kilter. It still went all the way on and at first glance, appeared okay, but if I were to tilt it, it would have leaked badly. It was a close-but-no-banana kind of thing. In horseshoes this would have been fine and good for points, but not in a drinking bottle, as they go by two totally different sets of rules. If I used it this way, every time I would take a drink, I would also be washing the front of my shirt. Though that was not a bad idea on some occasions, it was not what I wanted to do all day while at work. Maybe during an all-you-can-eat-ribs day at Texas Road House, but not here at my desk—not without a bib anyway. To use it as it was, would have been to use it in a way it was not designed.

The fix was easy, I just had to back up and start over. And that is what I did. I unscrewed it all the way off, put the lid back in place and this time the threads went into the right grooves, and all was well with the world again as far as my water jug was concerned.

Getting in the Groove

The word groove seems to be a good thing in general. It is a positive statement to say, "I am in the groove." They also cut grooves in roads to let water runoff while you are driving. So good there also. It's likewise a good thing when we say, "Hey, that's groovy," but at the same time, our kids look at us like, did you really talk that way? And we of course reply, "Right on, little man."

All this "groovy" talk reminds me of something most kids know nothing about . . . records. Not the kind you keep in a file or get when you go to jail. I am speaking of the giant 33 LPs that held the "out-of-sight" music in our day. Or even the little 45s that held a single song on either side of them. I actually still have a stack of 45s that I plan to use as wall decor in my studio.

For those of us that know what I am speaking of, you know that records have "grooves" in them. When a needle is placed in this groove on a spinning record player, the needle follows this groove and out comes bea . . . utiful music from the speakers. And it went on like this until the record started getting some scratches in it that were not a part of the groove.

At first you would just hear a little pop as the needle went by when the scratch was pretty minor. But sometimes the scratches got much worse. Usually, it was because the record was not well taken care of or sometimes because someone bumped the player on accident when it was going. Then you would get a deep scratch. This scratch would at least cause the song to jump ahead and if it was bad enough, cause it to fly right out of the groove and off the center of the record, leaving more scratches in its path. The more severe scratch made a sound that was very unique, demanded attention and caused you to clinch up a little while lifting your shoulders slightly and tightening down with your jaw muscles. It went something like . . . ZZZZRR-RIIIIPPPPXXXZZZSSSS. And unlike CDs of our current day, there was no repairing them.

A 30-Day Devotional

Have you ever been in the groove? Everything was going just right and things were looking so fine. Then it happened. Something came along and knocked you clean out of your groove and sent your life spiraling to the center of your record when just a second ago such beautiful music had been playing. You didn't see it coming. You didn't see any yellow flags or hear any warning sirens, but yet . . . WHAM . . . there you are.

Or maybe you were not so obviously knocked out of your groove, but just rather, one day found yourself not quite in the place you used to be and wanted to be. It was like a small scratch had changed things a little or maybe like the threads of your life had not quite lined up and you had been figuratively leaking but had not realized it. You thought things were okay, but somehow, you find yourself off the path you wanted to be on.

Life has a great way of doing this to us, doesn't it? We have all been there, will be there or maybe are there right now this very moment. I don't believe anyone escapes. The difference, I think, lies in our choice. We all don't bother to get back in the groove. Some of us just start a new groove and give up on the old groove, even though we know that we are not where we should be.

This life is a fight to the finish for sure and the right things and right ways will always be the harder things and harder ways. The wrong things in life do not take any work or effort and don't lead us anywhere except down or to the center of our records. As Christians, we have an enemy that the Bible says comes to steal, kill, and destroy. He seeks to steal our hopes, kill our dreams, destroy our witness. In short, he comes to scratch the record that is playing God's great song for our life. He wants it scratched so badly that we don't even try to play it anymore.

We also face an even more personal enemy. I think you know who it is. You have heard it said, "I have seen the enemy . . . and the enemy is ME." I can't speak for your life, but in my life, this is so true. If I dig into most cases of bad things happening in my life, I can almost always trace it back to me. It is almost al-

Getting in the Groove

ways rooted in my choices and my selfishness. Oh, it is easier to blame it on the devil and I'm sure he likes to help, but our flesh is a mighty foe even without his help.

And so, we fight this "Spirit versus Flesh" battle day in and day out, strengthened by the One we love and torn down by an enemy that hates us. Not a relaxing picture, is it?

We have quite a lot on our plates as Christians. So, what must we do? As a starting point, we must remember that we can always "unscrew our lid," so to speak, and start over. As long as we are still on this earth and have breath in our lungs, we can never go so far that we cannot stop, turn and go in the right direction. We must stop, do a 180 and turn from what we know we should not be doing and start again. It is as simple and as hard as that. It is called "repentance."

Furthermore, we must be aware of what we are a part of. We must be aware that our choices matter. We must be aware that things and people are impacted for the good or the bad by what we choose and do every day. We must choose to live differently and deliberately. Most importantly, we must choose clearly just whose side we are going to play for and quit riding the fence, maybe for the first time in our entire lives. We must cut from our lives all the things the Holy Spirit of God has been telling us to, instead of making excuses that have no foundation in anything except our selfishness. Do not doubt that God has a plan and a design for each and every one of our lives. But know that our freewill plays a big part in the outcome. Will we play His song for our lives or follow the scratches? We must choose.

Father, we have so many things trying to tell us which way we should go and attempting to pull us off the course You have set for our lives. And though I have made progress, there are still so many areas that, if I am honest, I cannot say I have surrendered totally to You. And if I have not given all to You, then how can I call You

A 30-Day Devotional

Lord of my life? Oh Father, please show me clearly those areas of my life that I have not fully given to You. Let Your Spirit shine on everything You desire for me to surrender to You. Give me the strength and the courage, my God, to hand them over freely. But if there are areas that I will not let go of, I give You permission to take them by force. Please be my Lord.

I love You,

David

John 10:10

The thief comes only to steal and kill and destroy; I have come that they may have life, and have it to the full.

Revelation 3:15-17

I know your deeds, that you are neither cold nor hot. I wish you were either one or the other! So, because you are lukewarm—neither hot nor cold—I am about to spit you out of my mouth. You say, 'I am rich; I have acquired wealth and do not need a thing.' But you do not realize that you are wretched, pitiful, poor, blind and naked.

Jeremiah 29:11-13

"For I know the plans I have for you," declares the Lord, "plans to prosper you and not to harm you, plans to give you hope and a future. Then you will call upon me and come and pray to me, and I will listen to you. You will seek me and find me when you seek me with all your heart."

In what areas of your life have you gotten out of the groove that you are supposed to be in?

Day 15

Burnt Toast

I pushed the lever down and went on with my morning routine. As I prepared my lunch for the day and got my coffee ready for the ride to work, my toast was busy getting its tan on. I had already fed my dog, Peanut, and was waiting expectantly for my toast to pop up. But for some reason, it was not popping up. WHY WAS IT NOT POPPING UP??? All of sudden, my mind smashed the glass and hit the panic button located at the top and to the left of my frontal lobe. The message was clear . . . it had been too long . . . way, way, too long. I sprang into action and responded like a ninja fireman to rescue my toast in distress.

I stood at the bottom of the toaster looking up and yelling, "JUMP, JUMP . . . we will catch you," as I and three volunteers held the mat that looked like a trampoline. Our knuckles were white as we gripped the edge of the mat ever so tightly with anticipation of the coming catch. But my commands were only answered by deafening silence, and I knew I was going to have to go in if my toast would have any chance at all.

Then all of a sudden, I heard it "POP" and the toast was up and out. A sigh of relief passed my lips as I wiped beads of sweat from my forehead. But the damage had been done. Though they were still alive, my two slices of bread were badly blackened, and it did not look good at all. In the distance and in a high voice I heard someone say, "It looks like they are toast."

Some might have held out no hope and just carelessly tossed them away. If it had not been for the childhood training I received as—well, as a child—I might have just tossed them out as a loss. But as luck would have it, one of my parents had shown me that burnt toast is not over until you say it is over.

As a child, they had showed me how by using only a knife, you could hold the toast over the sink and slowly scrape the black, burnt part off, layer by layer. And when you were done, what you would have was a pretty normal looking piece of bread, just a little bit skinnier. What most people saw as a lost cause, I saw as an opportunity for a second chance. And a second chance is what my two pieces of toast got.

With another successful resurrection behind me, peanut butter was spread, coffee was mugged, a lunch box was picked up and in a flash, I had disappeared into the darkness of the morning, never to be seen at that exact time or day again.

I can easily picture myself as burnt toast in this life. I once was burnt but now I'm brown, was toast but now I'm free. It is God's amazing grace that looked down on me in all my burnt-ness—in my uselessness and sinful self. When I was just a big loafer and would not rise to any occasion, when my life was just one big jam after another, God chose to reach down and scrape me clean. He chose to scrape me. When others could see no worth and would have just thrown me away, He picked me up and scraped away all the darkness from my life that this world had put on me. Talk about scraping by. Then I think He said, "As I have scraped you, so scrape one another." Isn't that in the Bible somewhere? You know, the whole-y Bible filled with the Bread of Life?

Burnt Toast

Oh Father . . . I love You so much for loving me even though I have often been a heel and treated You and those You have made, crummy at times. I thank You that You never, ever, give up on me or any of those You have made. I pray that Your love would rise up like yeast in my heart and that You would teach me to treat others the way You treat others. May my words not just be flour-y talk but rather may You empower me by Your Spirit to spread the wonder of Your love to everyone You put in my path.

Love, David

Romans 5:8 (NIV 1984)

But God demonstrates his own love for us in this: While we were still sinners, Christ died for us.

1 Samuel 16:7 (NIV 1984)

But the LORD said to Samuel, "Do not consider his appearance or his height, for I have rejected him. The LORD does not look at the things people look at. People look at the outward appearance, but the LORD looks at the heart."

When did God scrape away your blackness and restore you to perfect toastiness?

Day 16
The Construction of Life

The spring and fall are my most favorite times to ride my motorcycle. The weather is mild during these times of the year. Yes, it is a little chillier in the morning, but usually just perfect in the afternoon. My perfect temperature to ride is when it is in the low 80s. That temperature is my "Goldilocks" temperature. What is that you ask? Okay, I'll tell you. Not too hot . . . not too cold . . . ah, just right.

Last summer, I moved to the big (little) city of Nampa. This put me about nine miles farther than my old commute when I lived in Boise, bringing it up to about 24 miles. In great commute traffic, this only adds a few minutes to my old time because it is a lot more of the trip on the freeway. But after last summer, that all changed.

A 30-Day Devotional

It is a strange phenomenon when they start construction in Idaho. They don't just start in on one place and work on it until it is done. Instead, they (whoever "they" are) count to three and start everywhere at once, like it is a big race between all the places they are doing construction. At least it seems like that is their plan to me. And start everywhere is just what they did.

Recently, there was construction all along a 60-mile stretch from Boise to Fruitland. Overpasses were being torn down and new, bigger and better ones were slowly being built back up. New on-ramps and future lanes were being added in both directions while current driving lanes were being merged away to make room in the meantime. And even more, I believe that dogs and cats had begun living together. It was craziness at a high rate of crazy.

It was all so wrong, not in intent, but just because of it being all at the same time. It was also like driving a different way to work on the freeway every few days as traffic was moved from this lane to that and then back again. Sometimes they would cross me over the median to the other side of the freeway for a while and then next week bring the traffic from the other side over to my side. I was waiting for the big loop-to-loop or at least a sweet Hot Wheels style bank, but so far that has not come. It has been quite an undertaking this past year and though they are getting a lot done, they are far from being finished.

Sometimes I wonder if I am just a part of a big sociology study on how people react to various traffic conditions over a long period of time. Is there is cracking point? Is there a point of giving in to desperation? How does it affect my moods and my life in general knowing what I have to face on the way to and from work each day? But that can't be true; this isn't some kind of a Facebook experiment, is it? And deep in my annoyed heart, I do realize that SOMEDAY when this construction is all complete, I will be happy about most of what they have done—except the dogs and cats living together. But for now, I must learn to live

The Construction of Life

with the construction and face the fact that it will not be going away for a while.

All of this construction has really, really messed up my commute. It will bring traffic down to stop-n-go in two places in the morning on the way in and at least one place, but possibly three, on the way home.

All of this can double my normal commuting time. There are not many things I enjoy less than being in stop-n-go freeway traffic on my motorcycle for an extra thirty minutes each way to work. Sometimes I catch and smash bugs on my face shield just to feel like I am going fast, but even doing that, I usually can't fool me. It just sucks the joy right out of why I am riding my motorcycle in the first place—to ride at the speed of light, feeling wild and free with the wind blowing against my face and the occasional bug smashing on my face shield and me thinking, "He won't have the guts to do that again!" Yes, there is none of that in stop-n-go traffic and there is not much joy there either, I am afraid.

This has kept me from riding nearly as much as normal this summer. Today, I decided I was going to ride anyway, looking for alternate routes on side streets to bypass the bad parts of the freeway. I did do better today than if I would have taken the freeway, but I still added fifteen minutes to my commute.

The big plus was that I did not really have any stop-n-go traffic and so I did not have to catch and smash any bugs on my face shield. (Bugs everywhere cheering.)

What I am doing is searching for a different way to bring back my riding joy. I am accepting the fact that, for now, life as I used to know it has changed. When the construction is finally done, I will check out all the improvements and will most likely use them, but that will probably be next year. It may look familiar, or it may be completely different, I really don't know. I will just have to wait until it is completed to see. And then I will ride.

A 30-Day Devotional

I don't know about you, but this story is an example of what has been going on in my life the past few years. There have been so many changes. Everything that was what I considered, "normal," has been turned upside down. Storms have come and storms have gone, and some things have been washed away with the rain and will never return to the way they were before. With all the remolding of what my life is going to look like, during all this life construction, I have also lost some of my joy. I have grown tired, weary, weak at times and even discouraged.

Change is never easy for me nor for most people, but nevertheless it comes whether we like it or not. Because of the changes, I cannot go about life in the same way that I used to. Those roads have been closed while new roads are being built and my whole life seems to be under construction. The new normal is being set up and is starting to harden.

In the meantime, I am intentionally holding close to the ONE that knows everything about what is happening to me. The ONE that knew everything that was coming and the ONE that knows exactly what my life will be when it is all complete. With my Daddy's help, I search for new joy in the new things I am doing. And I put my trust in Him that when all the construction is done, when the last lanes of my life have been widened, when the final overpasses and on-ramps have all been completed, when the roads have been freshly paved and lines have been painted, that my life will flow more freely in a way that it never did before. That maybe my life freeway will be able to handle more traffic and I will be more useful to the ONE that matters most. Then I will say, thank You, Great Builder of my life.

Daddy, it's me . . . Your clay. I must confess that I do not always enjoy the molding process of my life. I must confess that there is pain in the change and a big part of me often just wants You to leave me as I am. And it is because of that part of me, I fight and complain so much. But I am also very much aware that I have no

The Construction of Life

idea what I really need in my life, to mold me into the best that You have for me. I know that You are the only One that has those plans, and so I trust You with all of Your changes for my life. I trust in Your love for me and that all You have ever wanted for my life is what is best for me. Though I am so very short sighted, You are not. I lay my life in Your hands, Great Lover of My Soul. Please give me the grace, love, and endurance that I need, to be all that You have made me to be in this life. And I will thank You in advance.

Love,

David

Isaiah 43:18-19

Forget the former things; do not dwell on the past. See, I am doing a new thing! Now it springs up; do you not perceive it? I am making a way in the wilderness and streams in the wasteland.

Isaiah 64:8

Yet you, Lord, are our Father. We are the clay, you are the potter; we are all the work of your hand.

What parts of your life are under construction? Have you caught the vision for what your new roads and paths will look like when you are finished?

Day 17
Sink or Swim

They were words that I would almost immediately live to regret. One of my daughters had just said to me, "Peanut wants to jump in, should we let her?" At the time, four of my daughters were in float tubes doing their float thing in Mann Creek Reservoir and our family dog, Peanut Butter Wood, was on Shelby's lap as she floated.

Now first, let's talk a little about Peanut Butter Wood. She is a purebred Chihuahua, but saying that, she is not as tiny as most of them. She is not tiny at all. She weighs about 11 pounds and though I would like to tell you that she is built like a brick, she is built more like a bag of marshmallows with a lot of attitude. If they made a hot and sassy brand of marshmallows, that would be a good picture of her. Lots of fluff with a little bite.

There she was, this fine specimen of a dog perched on the edge of a blow up tube, ready to take the plunge. My daughter, Kendra, was calling her and Peanut Butter Wood appeared to want to jump in and swim to her. And so, answering my daughter's question, I said, "All dogs know how to swim. If she wants to jump, let her."

After the words left my mouth, I stood on the shore 20 feet from it all and watched with bated breath. No one had ever actually seen Peanut Butter Wood swim, but she was certainly a dog, so what could go wrong? I was soon to find out the answer to that question.

As Kendra called, Peanut Butter Wood squatted, then paused, squatted, then paused and then . . . off she went. She was up about a foot above the water when she jumped and dove nose first and at a diving slant down. And just like that, she was gone. She went under the water like a pointy-nosed rock and disappeared from view. Shelby said all she could see was little bubbles going down about six feet.

At this point, great panic ensued. There was a loud commotion, and much splashing of water and loud shrieks were heard across the countryside. The girls were also making a lot of noise too. Kendra sprung from her float tube like a shark had just bit her on the butt. She immediately went under the water in search of Peanut Butter Wood. She came up the first time PBW-less with the intent to immediately go back down. But as she came up Peanut Butter Wood crawled her way up her body and on to her shoulder.

I was on the shore waiting for the search outcome and preparing myself to plunge deep into the creek if needed. I was glad to see Peanut Butter Wood perched on Kendra's shoulder. She was not afraid or shaking and just kind of looked at everyone like, "What is your guys' problem?"

Kendra paddled to shore and put the pup in shallow water, who then walked out to me. I picked her up and she seemed fine. She was not shaking and did not seem to be overly concerned about anything. She was wet and a little bit muddy and sandy but other than that, no worse for wear.

The girls seemed to be a little upset with me for telling them to let PBW jump, but really, everyone had just been very afraid. My

Sink or Swim

advice would have been the same under similar circumstances, as I have never met a dog who could not swim. And even now, I was not sure that PBW could not. She may just be an extraordinary, sleek diving dog more closely resembling a seal in the water, rather than a Chihuahua. She may have well been speeding her way to the surface after her dive and was ready to get some air and do a flip when she ran into Kendra. We really don't know for sure. All we do know is that it scared the bejeebers out of us, all because we could not see her and thought we had lost her forever.

We do have plans to let PBW try again if she wants, in my daughter, Ruthanne's, pool that she has set up in her backyard. That way, we can actually see her and see if we have the only dog that cannot swim or if we have a sleek swimming seal dog (SSSD). PBW actually went out on the tubes later with the girls and wanted to jump once again. But for some reason, they would not let her and they definitely did not ask DAD what he thought!!!

I have taken quite a few leaps in my years of life. Sometimes I have sunk right off the plank. Sometimes I have swum for a while, only to sink later. But every now and then, I have jumped and swum like a fish. The thing is, sometimes you don't know what you can and can't do if you never try. Cliff diving may be one of the exceptions in my mind. With that, I think you have to be good right from the start, or you may not get a second chance. But in general, besides cliff diving, I would much rather try something and fail at it, than sit back and never take a chance, watching life go by and wondering if I could have done it or not. There are many things I have tried, many things I am doing now, and I hope to try many more things in the future.

Here are two things I am currently doing: I am a writer of many songs and I hope to continue to write and record many more. I am also an author of one book with one more on the way. Both of these things are desires I feel God has put on my heart. And though I don't know if I am ever going to be able to make my living at them, I am still swimming hard and looking for what opportunities might open up. There are many ways to measure success and when I see one life touched, it gives me strength to keep trying—to keep swimming. And maybe that is all that God has in mind for these gifts . . . one person at a time. If that is true, is that so bad? I think not.

In summary, I do not want to get to the end of my life and regret not trying all the things that I wanted to try to do. I would much rather get to the end of my life full of all the funny, fun, and not so fun stories of things I tried but did not work and things I tried that did. I am okay with maybe even having a few bumps, bruises, and scars from all the living of life along the way. At the end of our lives, I think we will all see the remarkable, invaluable, precious gift of time that we were all given.

What about you? What would you like to do? What is holding you back? Are you ready to take the plunge? Life awaits.

Daddy, thanks so much for this gift of life that You have given me. And with Your gift of life comes a set amount of time to spend. Help me to see the precious value of this finite time before me as I spend it on this thing called, "My life." Help me to use it wisely and to spend it on valuable and worthy things. Help me, lead me, guide me, and teach me how to make the most of what You have given me.

Love,

David

Psalm 103:15-16

The life of mortals is like grass, they flourish like a flower of the field; the wind blows over it and it is gone, and its place remembers it no more.

Sink or Swim

Is there something that you should try that you have not done yet because fear of man, fear of failure, or fear of looking silly has held you back?

Day 18
The Making of Kitty Wampus

On the way to work today, in the rain, on the freeway, about five miles from my destination, the word "kittywampus" came into my head. I don't know how; I don't know why. Maybe it was a direct gift from God and maybe not. You can be the judge after reading more, as this word has sparked a plethora of thoughts in this crazy mind of mine.

I have not thought about this word for many, many moons—maybe more. I am not even sure where I heard this word, though I think my mom may have used it when I was a little child. And for some reason, here it is back in my mind today.

I thought I knew what it meant. I knew for sure what I thought it meant, which was something that was a little out of whack—not lined up right. When I got to work, I looked it up in several places just to check my proposed and learned meaning of the word. Below is what I found:

The Urban Dictionary:

1. Utter chaos, thrown together, unorganized in any sense.

2. *Crazy word from southwestern Wisconsin meaning off-balanced, uncentered, or general state of confusion.*

The Wiktionary Dictionary: *Slang from catawampus. Disorganized, poorly done, chaotic.*

Dictionary.com: *Catawampus: Adjective: askew, awry, positioned diagonally; cater-cornered. Adverb: diagonally; obliquely.*

Growing up, I knew what a "catty-corner" and "kitty-corner" was. We had a big console television that was placed catty-corner in our living room. So, I guess it was only natural and expected that I would hear the word, Kitty Wampus. Though I know these words and their meaning, I cannot help but wonder about their origin. So let's explore my thoughts on this. (Oh no!)

First off, cats and/or kitties are surely at the beginning of all of these words—spelling wise and figuratively speaking. Logic would say that the origin of these words has something to do with a cat and/or a kitty. Many words such as syndromes and diseases are named after a person. Lou Gehrig's disease and Gilbert Syndrome are a couple examples that jump out at me. And in my life, I have had many cats and kittens also jump out at me. Coincidence or direct link? You be the judge. So, could Kitty Wampus have been named in a similar way? Maybe it went something like this.

Once upon a time, there was a woman who had many cats. She may have lived upstairs and been over forty and rumored to be crazy. Several of her cats had a litter of kittens—kitties if you will (and even if you won't). Yes, she had lots of cats and lots of kitties for sure. Most of her cats and kitties looked pretty much the same as each other in structure, but they had many variations in color. All but two that is. Those two had physical characteristics different from the rest of the cats and kitties and also different from each other.

The Making of Kitty Wampus

The mommy cat's name was She-lean and the baby kitty's name was Wampus. She-lean's two left legs were shorter than her two right legs or maybe her two right legs were longer than her two left legs. Both descriptions of She-lean appeared to be true no matter which angle or view you looked from. No matter the perspective, this surely made She-lean see the world from a slightly different angle than the other cats.

Kitty Wampus was different from his mommy. Though he had two legs that were shorter or two legs that were longer just like his mommy, they were not on the same side. Kitty Wampus' left front leg and back right leg were the shorter ones. Or maybe it was the back left and front right legs were longer. Both descriptions of Kitty Wampus appeared to also be true. When Kitty Wampus walked, he kind of had an up and down motion to his stride which caused him to see the world at a very different and changing angle from his mom. Though different from each other, they both saw the world differently from the rest of cats and kitties.

And of course, all the other cats saw She-lean and Kitty Wampus as outcasts because of their different angles of life. When they would walk by, they would make snide cat/kitty comments, making fun of how She-lean and Kitty Wampus walked. At times, some would even imitate them, "Hey look at me, I am Kitty Wampus" as they walked as if their legs were not the same length. And over time as the teasing continued, when something in a cat's life was not lined up right, was crooked or topsy-turvy, they just began to say it was "Kitty Wampus."

As humans, it seems like we have the propensity to point out and often ridicule things that are different from what we perceive as normal and/or things that we don't understand. I experienced some of this myself growing up.

There is a trait that ran in my family. My granddaddy had them, my daddy had them, and then they were honorably and ceremonially passed down to me. That trait was larger than life and outstanding to say the least or maybe more correctly . . . standing out. In fact, the trait that was passed down was unusually large ears that stuck out from my head. My sister was the first born and did not have them. My brother was next and did not have them. I was last and boom, there they were, right there on the side of my head. You could not miss them—even from one hundred yards in dim lighting.

As a baby and toddler, looking back at pictures, they were cute. But as I got a little older, they were not so adorable anymore. I began to be teased in school by other kids and called one name I remember in particular—Dumbo. Yes, the Disney character elephant with the extra big floppy ears. Even at home, I faced some teasing. I still remember my brother saying I looked like a VW Bug driving down the street with all its doors open. I did think it was funny, but at the same time, just because something is funny, does not mean it is not hurtful. And that was the case with me.

In second grade things got worse. I began to get into fights at school because of the names and the teasing. My mom worked for a plastic surgeon and though it was not a common practice like it is today, my mom and dad got my ears "pinned back." Actually, it was more complicated than that; they also reduced the overall size by taking off the original curl of my ears and forming a new curl.

I guess I am famous in a way. Pictures of my before and after ears were in a medical book touting a successful procedure. There were some complications that required painful shots for some time but all in all, for the time it was a great success. The goal was accomplished. I was no longer a target of teasing because of my different appearance.

I have thought about what would have happened had I not had that procedure. I am sure the teasing would have continued and so would my reactions to it. I wonder if I would have just gotten callused and eventually unaffected by the teasing. Or maybe my

The Making of Kitty Wampus

humor would have risen up as a defense to diffuse the teasing. Or maybe I would have just become a great fighter and would have hurt people before they could try to hurt me. I think it could have went any number of ways or settled somewhere in between. Maybe I would have been a callused funny guy who sometimes beat people up for seemingly no apparent reason. I may have even picked up a great nickname because of it all. Maybe someone like, David Funnyguy Kickurbuttus.

You see, we are affected by things that happen to us growing up and often those things stick to us as adults. Here I am at fifty-five years young, and these memories are still right on the tip of my memories. Everything we go through molds us one way or another—some for good and some for bad. Sometimes we begin to build walls to protect us and/or to hide behind. Sometimes we become people that we really are not, just to fit in better with the rest of the people in our lives—trying not to stand out. What I know for sure is growing up can be hard and people can be mean. That seems to be a constant truth even now as I watch kids growing up. Unfortunately, things have not changed.

In this big, big world we live in, we don't all look the same, think the same, or see the world the same way. We have many, many views and many, many perspectives. We react from truth and lies. We react from pleasure and pain. In all of our differences, deep down we are all a part of the human race, but also, we are each individually unique. God did not make us a cookie cutter creation for sure. We are all created in God's image and His masterpieces—big ears or not—long legs or short legs. Or like the old commercial used to say, "Fat kids, skinny kids, kids that climb on rocks, tough kids, sissy kids, even kids with chicken pox." Even though this was a commercial to sell Armour hot dogs, the lyrics are full of labeling all different kinds of kids (who loved hot dogs).

As I consider the thoughts that are flowing from my mind, through my fingertips and on to this paper, I am a little disheartened. I

A 30-Day Devotional

know that if a jingle like that was to play today, there would be an uproar from several groups, complaining about the song shaming different kids. But in truth, when you peel back all the political correctness, not much has really changed these days. Sure, we have made all these new rules to try to take care of all kinds of discrimination, yet it still remains. I have heard about the same kind of things I dealt with all those years ago continuing now with my grandchildren. I think it's because all the rules in the world cannot change the condition of the human heart. Only God can do that.

How would it be if we could see past these temporary bodies we all live in, right to the other person's soul? The same soul that is being crushed and damaged when we are cruel to one another or blossoming and growing when we are kind and loving. How wonderful that would be for sure.

The bad news is, most of the time we just see skin deep. It's so much easier to be superficial and shallow at times and push others down so we can feel lifted up. We find flaws in others so we can feel somewhat better about ourselves.

The good news is that it will not always be this way. One day we will shed these bodies and live in the presence of the One that sees us all exactly how we are—the One that looks at us and sees right to the depth of our souls—the One we can never ever hide anything from—the same One that loves us all so much and longs to be in relationship with us—the same One that wants to make us into the best "us'" we can be with His help and guidance—the very same One that made each and every one of us and made us all to fit into the Body of Christ perfectly. Someday, we will see how it is supposed to be—what we are really made to be. It will be awesomely beautiful. Oh, Father, I can't wait.

Daddy, it is not a surprise to You when I tell You that my thinking and actions can often be "Kitty Wampus." At times I lean to the left and at times I lean to the right. At times I have let myself be tossed

The Making of Kitty Wampus

like a wave of the sea and I am amazed that You still see the best in me. So today, now again, I ask that You would open my eyes to things that I currently do not see and close my eyes to things that get in the way of me seeing You clearly. I ask that You would grow me into someone that currently I am not and lay to rest the parts of me that keep me from moving closer into Your shadow. Help me not to ask for You to be with me, but rather, teach me to be with You. And I will thank You in advance, Great Lover of My Soul.

Love,

David

1 Samuel 16:7

But the Lord said to Samuel, "Do not consider his appearance or his height, for I have rejected him. The Lord does not look at the things people look at. People look at the outward appearance, but the Lord looks at the heart."

John 15:12

My command is this: Love each other as I have loved you.

Ephesians 4:32

Be kind and compassionate to one another, forgiving each other, just as in Christ God forgave you.

Romans 12:4-5

For just as each of us has one body with many members, and these members do not all have the same function, so in Christ we, though many, form one body, and each member belongs to all the others.

Psalm 91:1-2

Whoever dwells in the shelter of the Most High will rest in the shadow of the Almighty. I will say of the Lord, "He is my refuge and my fortress, my God, in whom I trust."

Have you ever judged someone for being "Kitty Wampus"? How would your view of people change if you looked past the outward appearance?

Day 19

Go Fly a Kite

Last weekend I was out in the country on my way to get my haircut. As I was driving, a big kite flying off to my left caught my attention. As I looked, I noticed it was in the shape of an airplane. It was also in trouble.

As I watched it, it was already in a slow "death spin," caused, in my experience, from not having enough weight on the tail. The older I have gotten, the heavier my tail has become and because of that, I have not done the "death spin" and crashed to the ground out of control for some time. I do occasionally have trouble lifting my tail end off the couch, but all good things have their downside. But this kite surely did not have enough junk in the trunk and because of this, down it went in the field it had just been looking down on, not so long before.

After the kite crashed, I followed the string all the way back to the holder and was expecting to find a kid at the other end. But to my surprise, this was no kid. The man holding the reel of string was probably close to my age! My take on the situation was that he was just an older gentleman enjoying the excitement and freedom of flying a kite. It reminded me that you never get too old for some things in life, and kite flying was probably one of those things for him.

It made me wonder if flying that kite brought him back to a time in his life when he was just a young lad; running free and wild. Did it take him back to a time when he did not have a care in the world? And now as an adult, maybe the cares and troubles of this old world fade away as he watches his kite soar higher and higher in the freedom of the wind, leaving everything below farther and farther behind.

Flying a kite and life seem to have many similarities to me. On one extreme, there have been times in my life where I have been soaring so high and things seemed so good and were going so well. Magical music played as my soundtrack of life as butterflies by day and fireflies by night, danced around my blessed life. The love of life oozed from every pore of my being.

On the other extreme, there have been times, many times actually, where things have gone quickly out of control and I found myself in a "death spin" that sent me crashing down to this hard, unforgiving earth. In these times, my magical music soundtrack of life was a single trumpet playing "Taps" while bats replaced my butterflies and fireflies and despair was now the cry of my heart.

I think that every one of us can relate to that analogy and if you can't, then just wait around until you turn three and check again. Life is not always smooth sailing and like an elevator, a pogo stick, ice skating, or a spring rocking horse it surely will have many ups and downs along the way.

Looking back over my life, surveying the highs and lows and all the in between, I think the key in all situations was in WHO I allowed to hold my string. You have heard the saying, "Looking for love in all the wrong places?" In my case, it was, "Giving my string to all the wrong places." We can give our string to so many things and so many people that we are being pulled in

Go Fly a Kite

too many directions. We don't even know if we are coming or going, are on our way, coming back, have already been there, or are visiting for the first time. We are being tossed like a wave of the sea, because we have no clear direction, just a bunch of opinions pulling us here and there, and none of them from the right place.

It is vital that the one we allow to hold the string of our lives is someone we can trust. It needs to be someone who is worthy of such a task and we know for sure has our best interest in mind. If we give that string to another person, to educational opportunities, our career, our financial security, or to ourselves—trusting no one else, it will fail and we will crash.

I'm not saying that you cannot spend time in the air with any of the above plans, but what I am saying is that all of them will fail you. None of the examples are dependable all the time and all will have their ups and downs. They will all change with current trends, popularity, culture, or simply with time. We can partner with people, but we must be tied to God. If we are allowing someone to pull our string in another direction, we must correct that. We must not make that same mistake. People worth hanging with are people who encourage you to keep your string in the hands of the only ONE who should have it.

There is only ONE that is the same yesterday, today, and forever. There is only ONE that does not change with the current trends, popularity, or culture. Simply and directly put, there is only ONE that can be trusted to hold our string. This same ONE gave HIS life for us, gave HIS everything for us, and gave HIS all for the very chance for us to give ourselves to HIM. He is the Christ, the Son of the Living God, He is the I Am and the One and only Savior of the World. He is Jesus.

On Good Friday every year, we remember when Jesus gave Himself up freely to be beaten, crucified, and die for our sins. On the following Sunday morning, we celebrate Easter, remembering that He rose from the dead in ultimate victory, proving who HE was and is—our King and our Savior.

Considering His great love and sacrifice for us, can we now consider giving only Him the string of our lives? Can we cut away anything and everything that pulls that string in another direction? Can we draw boundaries and develop protection that keep us close to Jesus and make Him first in our lives? Can we not just read His words but move them from our head to our heart and actually become and live out His words? May it be so oh LORD!

Consider the beautiful words from the song, *In Christ Alone* by Stuart Townsend and Keith Getty.

In Christ Alone

(Stuart Townsend and Keith Getty 2002, first verse)

In Christ alone my hope is found

He is my light, my strength, my song

This Cornerstone, this solid ground

Firm through the fiercest drought and storm

What heights of love, what depths of peace

When fears are stilled, when strivings cease

My Comforter, my All in All

Here in the love of Christ I stand

Daddy, I am humbled when I think of all that was done so I can talk directly to You this very moment. When I think that You gave Your Son for me and that You, Jesus, would agree to lay down Your very life for one such as me, I am just at a loss of words that are spectacular enough to express my feelings. So with that, I ask

Go Fly a Kite

You instead to listen to the words of my heart. I will never fully understand Your great love for me while I sit on this side of eternity. I give You my string now and ask that You alone fly me safely home to You. I love You and thank You.

Love,

David

James 1:5-8

If any of you lacks wisdom, you should ask God, who gives generously to all without finding fault, and it will be given to you. But when you ask, you must believe and not doubt, because the one who doubts is like a wave of the sea, blown and tossed by the wind. That person should not expect to receive anything from the Lord. Such a person is double-minded and unstable in all they do.

John 15:4

Remain in me, as I also remain in you. No branch can bear fruit by itself; it must remain in the vine. Neither can you bear fruit unless you remain in me.

John 14:20

On that day you will realize that I am in my Father, and you are in me, and I am in you.

Is Christ the one holding your string today? If not, in what directions are you being pulled?

Day 20
Rolling With De Papa

Recently, my wife, Denice, and I, took on an adventure. We decided to take three of our grand kids, Aidan, Anna, and Andrew, ages 9, almost 7 and 6, to the Nampa Rollerdrome in Nampa, Idaho, to go roller-skating. This would not be that big of a deal except none of the three had ever learned to roller-skate.

Our daughter, Kendra, momma to Andrew who is the 6-year-old, also went with us as well as our daughter, Billi, who was our official photographer and videographer to document possibly our last good deed on this earth.

When we got there, Kendra took her son, Andrew, Denice took Anna, and I took Aidan. We checked out the appropriate size skates, laced and strapped them on, locker'd up all our extra apparel and took off for the big oval.

A 30-Day Devotional

It is amazing how we take something that we can do for granted. I have been skating for as long as I can remember, maybe even longer. To this day there is a legend of a baby boy born in Wilmington, North Carolina that came out of the womb skating, to the surprise, amazement, and delight of the doctors, nurses, and hospital staff. Sadly, not everyone likes and can appreciate a newborn on skates. But anyway, my point is that skating is fairly natural for me and seeing someone now learning to skate for the first time made me appreciate my legendary skills.

The first half hour of learning to skate was what I can only describe as "extremely brutal!" The boys were down 97.5 percent of the time and the 2.5 percent of the time that they were up includes the time they were falling but had not yet hit the ground again.

Anna's time was not as bad, because she was more interested in doing what I can only describe as, "gliding," rather than skating. She was on skates and rolling, but her forward movement was due to whom she was holding onto or the wall, which she used to pull herself along and hold her upright.

The boys were not very interested in "gliding," They both wanted to learn how to skate, even if it killed them (and there were times when I wondered if it just might). Both of them wanted as little help as possible and they both paid dearly for their choice—in bruises.

In the beginning, I showed Aidan that I could hold him up and for the most part, keep him from falling. I say, "for the most part," because there was one fall that took us both down flat on our backs because he grabbed my arm as he was falling and I had seriously underestimated how much bigger he had gotten. Aidan did not want me to just keep him up, because that would keep him from learning. He did however, graciously accepted my help when he fell, to help him back on his feet and steady him before releasing him for his next try. In general, I stayed very close to him so he could grab on to me if he so chose. When

Rolling With De Papa

he fell, I offered my help and I blocked for him so he would not be run over by other skaters. Andrew and Kendra functioned much in the same manner.

Over the next two hours, there was a lot of determination, frustration, sweat and a few tears. With trial and error, over time something strange began to happen. The instructions and encouragement I had been giving Aidan all along began to transform from just empty words into real life application. He began to have moments where he saw them alive and in action as he was truly "skating."

Instead of his skates just continually rolling out from under him showing him the familiar view of the ceiling, he began to actually balance and push forward, creating momentum all on his own. It was true, he was actually beginning to skate.

As he began to skate more and more, he began to fall less and less. And the longer he stayed up, the bigger his smile got, as did mine. As Aidan got better, I gave him more and more space and freedom. But even though he did not realize it, I was still always close enough to be there and help him if and when he fell.

There were times when I would see him losing his balance and I would skate up alongside and just grab on to him until he was steady again. Then I would ask him if he was good and when he said yes, I would let go and fade away. Sometimes when he was threatening to fall, I would skate up right behind to catch him only to have him recover and so I would back off again. Many times he never even knew I was there watching over him.

In the end when it was time to leave, both Aidan and Andrew could both say they could now skate. They were not experts by any means, but they had come so far and had built a solid foundation on which to build upon in the future.

As their Papa Dave, I was so proud of them for what they had accomplished, but most of all for NOT GIVING UP. In all honestly,

I expected both of them to get frustrated with the whole thing, say it was dumb and turn in their skates. But I was so wrong and their determination to stick it out no matter what, speaks of the great character hidden in both of them even at this young age. There are certain kind of things in life that I don't mind being proved wrong on and this was certainly one of them. This one made me very proud to be wrong.

As for my granddaughter, Anna, I was also proud of her, but her experience was very different from the boys and an example perhaps for another story on another day.

The application on how this all reflects our relationship with our Heavenly Father is pretty straightforward and only hidden if you refuse to look.

As we roll along through this life, learning one new thing after another, as we face things that stretch us to our snapping point, we must remember that we, like Aidan and Andrew are never alone. We might feel like we are at times, but it is just not true.

Our Heavenly Father is right there skating along with us as we roll through this life, continually offering us His words of instruction and encouragement. He is there to help us get back up on our feet and steady us if we will just let Him. He is even there with us when we have fallen flat on our back and are looking up at the ceiling, so to speak. God told us that He would never leave or forsake us. He did not say, "Sometimes I will leave you and every now and then, I will forsake you." He said, NEVER and that means . . . well . . . never. We are never out of the sight, care, and protection of our PAPA.

We are truly never on our own, but that does not mean we don't have much to learn. We have absolutely tons to learn, there is no doubt. God has plans for us and as we allow Him to, He will put them in front of our wheels and then away we will skate.

Rolling With De Papa

The road may be hard or it may be easy. It may have high hills and deep valleys. It may have tight turns with big drop offs and gnarly jumps. But if He has set it before us, if we can just accept that when we are done with all the falls, crashes, and crunches, in the end—if we do not give up—we will not be the same people we were before we started. We will be skating in ways we did not think we could before. We will roll on to see God's words of instructions and encouragement come alive and active in the reality of our lives as we live out His truth. And that, my skaters, will be sweet. And coolest of all, our Great Heavenly Papa will roll right next to us and say, "I'm so proud of you. Roll on my child."

Papa, thank You so much for never leaving us alone. Thank You that You care about all aspects of my life and offer me Your guidance and encouragement when I choose to take it. Thank You that even when I am hard-headed, stubborn and self-centered, and choose my own hard way, You are still there with me and even work those times out for my best in the long run. Thank You for all You have taught me, are teaching me now, and will teach me in the future.

Love,

David

Deuteronomy 31:6&8

Be strong and courageous. Do not be afraid or terrified because of them, for the Lord your God goes with you; he will never leave you nor forsake you. The Lord himself goes before you and will be with you; he will never leave you nor forsake you. Do not be afraid; do not be discouraged.

Matthew 28:20b

"And surely I am with you always, to the very end of the age."

Romans 8:28

And we know that in all things God works for the good of those who love him, who have been called according to his purpose.

James 1:22-24

Do not merely listen to the word, and so deceive yourselves. Do what it says. Anyone who listens to the word but does not do what it says is like someone who looks at his face in a mirror and, after looking at himself, goes away and immediately forgets what he looks like.

Hebrews 4:12

For the word of God is alive and active. Sharper than any double-edged sword, it penetrates even to dividing soul and spirit, joints and marrow; it judges the thoughts and attitudes of the heart.

Are you aware that He is with you, even in the darkest night? How have you seen the Lord help you back up when you fall?

Day 21

One Bun or Two?

On Palm Sunday, a few years ago, while attending Valley Christian Church in Fruitland, Idaho, I had an incredible thought—a revelation even.

Now I would like to tell you that this epiphany was inspired by the awesome music or possibly the communion meditation that morning. Or maybe that it was inspired by the great love of the people shown there or the fantastic message preached by my friend, Ralph, that Sunday. But the truth is, although all of those things were true, it had nothing to do with any of them.

After leading music that morning, I had gone back to my seat in the second row next to my wife and my Grandma Cracker. Our friend Teresa had sat in the front row because there was no more room in our row. She had played keyboard with us that morning and since this was her first time at this church, I did not want her to have to sit there all alone. So I leaned over and told my wife I was going to sit with Teresa and moved up a row.

What happened next can only be described as a realization and unveiling of a great truth that had been hidden from me my whole life. Though it was not religious in the slightest, it was still deeply moving and significant in its own way.

When I moved up, I didn't want to just sit right next to Teresa, so I moved over to what I thought was an "acceptable" one seat between us boy/girl spacing. But I mis-sat and landed with only a half of a seat space between us. I did not want to distract further, so I decided to stay in my halfway position until a time arose that I could shift stealthily.

This does not sound like much on its own, but this positioning had left my left butt cheek on the left chair and my right butt cheek on the right chair. At the same time that I had realized my positioning error, I also realized that it was actually very comfortable. My new found comfort made me an instant "sitting rebel" and I stayed put in the "One Bun Per Chair" position ("OBPC" for those acronym lovers like myself) until the end of the service.

The support was awesome and I felt this new position fit my derrière so much better than the traditional "Two Buns Per Chair" (TBPC) position I had come to believe was the only way to sit in a chair. In one bun misplacement, my sitting world traditions had been turned upside down.

Why didn't we all sit like this? Had this ever been tried before? Was this some kind of church conspiracy that was being kept from us on purpose so "they" could keep it all to themselves? Should we set up a church with both kinds of chairs and let the people choose? Did Jesus and the Apostles sit like this? Did I remember to turn off the coffeepot this morning? Many, many very important questions were running through my head.

An old saying full of wisdom that I'm sure must be in my Bible somewhere came to me. Maybe it was just written on a sticky note stuck in my Bible but, "technically" that is still in my Bible. The words said, "Don't let the door hit you where the good Lord split you."

One Bun or Two?

Yes, it was true. God, the Creator of the universe, the Maker of you and me, the same One that strung the stars in the sky and made the mountains, forests, and trees had split us in that very place and now we were trying to deny His divine creation by using chairs that insulted his wonderful insight. We were obviously fighting God's perfect design with all of our human stubbornness. It was all becoming so clear to me—so perfectly clear.

I now saw this as ridiculous as us wearing a baseball cap with two humps for our one hump head or pants with only one leg for our two legs or dogs and cats living together in this imperfect, crazy, mixed-up world! Yes, as the truth began to sink in, I knew I had been deeply changed and I would never, ever, be the same again. (Dramatic music plays here.)

Life, it seems, works very much in this way. I know what you are thinking. Whatcha talkin' 'bout, Willis? Well, let me pull it all together for you.

First, let me start with this. There are some things that will never, ever, change. There are absolute things that are right and absolute things that are wrong and solid truths—things that don't change with time, culture, temperature, humidity, altitude, underwater, under duress, or just our whims. They are foundational truths that remain the same, no matter how much some people may want to change them at times.

Our God is the same yesterday, today, and forever. Our God is the One and only God, not just another god among the thousands of other little-g gods and all the other things we so foolishly worship.

Jesus was, is, and always will be the only way to His Father. He stated clearly that no one comes to His Father except through Him. Jesus came and died on the cross for our sins and was raised from the dead by the Holy Spirit and the only way to salvation is through grace by accepting what was done for us on the cross. There is nothing more that we can add to what has already been done for us.

Salvation is a free gift given to us because of the great love God has for us and because He wants to have a close, personal relationship with us. It CANNOT be earned. There was no way for us to do it in ourselves, so our Abba Father made a way through His Son. Then He gave us the Holy Spirit to help us, comfort us, lead us, guide us, and teach us to be more like His Son.

These are just a few things off the top of my head that are unchanging and immovable truths.

How we sit, where we sit, what we wear, what we don't wear, do we raise our hands, do we not raise our hands, do we jump to the left, or do we jump to the right, are not set in stone. How we pray, where we pray, and when we pray is something that is probably different for every one of us and a personal thing between us and God.

There are no formulas for what makes many things "right" or "wrong" though we are constantly searching for one. Each relationship with God is unique and God does things exactly like He wants to, not like we want Him to. The sooner we get over that, the better we will be and the sooner we can begin to learn what trust and faith truly is.

Is one kind of music more holy than another or are the different styles just different offerings from each generation? Does God delight in one style or one kind of thing, but not the other? We can drive ourselves absolutely loony with questions that don't really matter in the big scheme of things.

I don't think it is the "what" that is being offered that is the important thing. I think the worthiness of any gift that we offer and give to God to honor Him is not found in the object itself, style, or tradition, but rather ONLY in the INTENT OF THE HEART of the one offering it. That, I believe, is what is most important!

One Bun or Two?

In summing this all up, we need to be focusing on loving each other inside AND outside the church so that people will see the love of God clearly. If the church loved the world like Jesus did, our biggest problem would be finding places for all the people to sit. Instead, they watch us gossip, bicker, and tear each other apart over dumb things and wonder why they would ever want to be a part of that. We don't want them asking, "So that's love?"

We need to hold fast to the foundational truths of God. We must stand boldly against anything that lowers who we know God is and attempts to lift us up to who we are not. Make no mistake; we are NOTHING without God . . . NOTHING!

We must also not get weighed down with the rules and opinions that man and tradition may try to put on us. Isn't that what happened to the Pharisees? We remember the words Jesus had for the rule-following Pharisees and we don't want to be anything like them. Do we? Not unless you like being called, "Whitewashed tombs filled with dead men's bones."

Most importantly, I think we need to keep our heart open to God and be willing to do things that are out of our comfort zones if God asks us to. We may even need to be willing to do things that may go against how we have always done it. "How we have always done it" may be holding us back from something God has for us, something bigger, better, something greater, and maybe even scarier. Who knows, it may just start with picking up the remote, turning off the TV, and getting off the couch.

Real change and growth only come when we are willing to open ourselves up to God working on and with us. But as always, the choice is up to you and to me. Are you ready?

Oh Daddy, I can look back on my life and see that You have certainly grown me over the years, but at the same time, I am keenly aware that time is fleeting and there is much to be done. Please open my eyes, lead me, and guide me by Your Holy Spirit away from my selfish goals and instead to the ways, thoughts, and places that are fully in Your view.

Love,

David

Hebrews 13:8

Jesus Christ is the same yesterday and today and forever.

Matthew 23:27-28

"Woe to you, teachers of the law and Pharisees, you hypocrites! You are like whitewashed tombs, which look beautiful on the outside but on the inside are full of the bones of the dead and everything unclean. In the same way, on the outside you appear to people as righteous but on the inside you are full of hypocrisy and wickedness."

John 14:6

Jesus answered, "I am the way and the truth and the life. No one comes to the Father except through me."

Isaiah 55:8-9

"For my thoughts are not your thoughts, neither are your ways my ways," declares the Lord. "As the heavens are higher than the earth, so are my ways higher than your ways and my thoughts than your thoughts."

One Bun or Two?

Is God asking you to do something different from what you have always done? Are you trusting Him to know what is best for you?

Day 22
The Source of Course

God often shows me something in the simplest things in life. That is what happened again last week while getting ready for work.

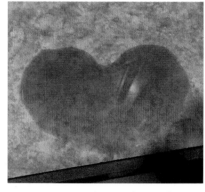

I have a little routine in the morning while getting ready to leave for work. I do all my bathroom events and after the scores come in from the judges, I move on to the kitchen floor events. This is where God decided to teach me that day.

I put my lunch together, filled my water bottle, put two pieces of toast into the toaster, and went to mug my coffee. Now, just to be clear, I do not mean I had someone hold my coffee's arms behind their back while I punched them in the stomach and stole their wallet. I am more boringly just referring to pouring my coffee into a travel mug . . . thus, mugging my coffee.

A 30-Day Devotional

The mugging of the coffee is usually close to the last thing I do. If I go too fast while pouring the coffee, liquid shifting voodoo happens and coffee will miss my mug somehow. Most of the time I do remember this, but every now and then, I still go too fast and make a mess.

This morning was a "go too fast" morning and as I finished filling up my mug, I noticed a circle of coffee on the floor. My first reaction was to dab up the coffee with a paper towel. That worked great, but after I cleaned it up and looked back a few moments later, it was back there again. Under closer inspection, I saw coffee dripping down the front of the cabinet drawers and following it upward, I found the source, a much bigger circle of coffee on the countertop.

I could have just keep wiping up the floor but that would not have stopped the problem that was coming from the source. Instead, I would have just been dealing with the symptoms or consequences. So first I went and dabbed up all the coffee on the countertop which stopped the flow of coffee, then cleaned up what was running down the face of the cabinet and then finally, finished up with the floor, thus eliminating the problem from this incident for good. Any other order would have made me have to do the same work over again.

As I was wiping up the coffee, thoughts of life began to come. Yes, life is like spilled coffee I guess—or at least in my crazy mind it is. Forest Gump says, "Life is like a box of chocolates" and I say, "Life is like spilled coffee on the counter, running down the cabinet and onto the floor." Sure, Forest's saying flows a little better, but this is not about flow, people. Oh wait, maybe it is about flow—coffee flow and life flow. Ha!

In this life, I have observed in myself and others, situations that are much like my spilled coffee on the floor. Over and over a situation is wiped up, but it always seems to come back and no one seems to know why. Over and over, it plays out the same way. Life spills and the resulting mess is cleaned up once again.

The Source of Course

And around and around we go, never knowing, never growing, never looking deeper for the source of our reoccurring pain and disappointment.

I have heard a definition for insanity is doing the same thing over and over and expecting a different outcome. Real change does not come until we are ready to make hard choices to move us to a different place. Real change does not come until we realize that we may be our biggest problem and our biggest enemy. You have heard the saying, "I have seen the enemy . . . and the enemy is me." Maybe just maybe, we are sabotaging ourselves out of fear of change.

Change is hard and change takes bravery and determination. We must be fed up enough to choose it and then strong enough to do whatever it takes to see it through to the end. It is there that we will be changed and conquer a problem at its source.

It is much easier to make excuses for why we can't do something and why things are like they are, instead of making decisions to correct situations we know are not good and healthy for us. It is much easier to stay where we are and dig a hole for our heads in the sand than to deal with something we do not like about ourselves—a situation we want to change or a problem that plagues us. In the end, change will start or not start with us.

If we choose to make changes in our lives that make a positive difference, we may even find that we will begin to pour life a little more slowly and cautiously. We may even find ourselves thinking of the consequences our choices have on ourselves and those around us, even BEFORE we do something, instead of always trying to clean up afterward, thus avoiding much pain and sorrow. That would be an awesome place to be for sure. Lord, make it so!

Father, please help me see past myself. Help me see through my excuses and to identify and heal me of my blind spots. Show me where I need to tear down my faulty construction and help me in the demolition. Then please build me into something that is valuable and useful to those that You have put in my life.

Love,

David

Luke 6:45

A good man brings good things out of the good stored up in his heart, and an evil man brings evil things out of the evil stored up in his heart. For the mouth speaks what the heart is full of.

Hebrews 12:15

See to it that no one misses the grace of God and that no bitter root grows up to cause trouble and defile many.

What areas in your life are the source of your spilled coffee? Have you looked at the hurts and sins that have led to your symptoms?

Day 23
Knock, Knock . . . Who's There?

I heard a comedian many years ago run through a routine that I would call, "Alice Doesn't Live Here Anymore." I do not remember who it was, but for some reason it struck me as very funny and has stuck with me all these years and I expect it to stick with me all the way to heaven. I will probably do it for whoever picks me up when I die and they will most likely roll their eyes, mutter under their angel breath, and wonder, "Why me?"

I know you guys and gals are now all dying for me to give it up and tell you WHAT exactly I am talking about. I know your curiosity has to be eating at you like a starving man would eat at a piece of bacon blown his way from a nearby Jack in the Box in a windstorm. If you are Jewish, no worries, you can substitute a piece of lamb for the bacon to keep this visual going for you. Yes, I know, I am easy to work with.

A 30-Day Devotional

What happened was this: The comedian had a piece of wood in one hand and announces, (Insert cool voiceover of your choice here) "And now a scene from the movie, Alice Doesn't Live Here Anymore." Then without further ado, he made a fist and knocked on the piece of wood like it was a door. Then he waited, and then did it again, this time saying, "Alice?" Then he paused and then again knocked and said louder, "Alice, are you home?" This went on progressively finally ending with him asking someone who he pretended was walking by, "Have you seen Alice?"

I know what you are thinking and yes, you are a little dumber now after taking the time to read that. But if you had actually seen it, you might just think it was rather funny and a good ice breaker. When things get tense some time, try it. Stand up with something to knock on or by a table or wall and say, "And now, a scene from the movie, Alice Doesn't Live Here Anymore" and then go into the rest of the routine. I can pretty much guarantee the ice will surely be broken when you are done. I have done this on occasion and it has never, ever, failed me. I do not recommend this at a bar mitzvah, during a group prayer meeting, or at a convention for "The Honeymooner's Show." The latter might start a riot and you might end up, "On the moon." But if you do, you might use that time productively and see if Ralph ever made good on his threats and Alice is actually up there.

This all strangely enough, reminds me of a verse in Revelation. I know you are now hoping that I am referencing the "end times" and that this story will soon be over but sorry, no such luck. I am talking about Revelation 3:20 where, if I may paraphrase, we find Jesus, the Son of God and our Savior, knocking on the door of our heart. And further we find Him telling us that if we will just open the door, He will come in faster than a Kirby vacuum salesman (hopefully he will not toss dirt on your rug to show you just how good his vacuum is) and we can eat together.

Eating seems to have been a big thing back then. Whenever there was a get together, you find the people eating together.

Knock, Knock... Who's There?

Think of the last supper. Okay, you got it? We don't remember that as, "The Last Big Meeting" or "The Final Conference with JC and the Boys." We remember it by a food title, "The Last Supper." It makes me wonder if the disciples thought they were not going to get supper anymore after that night, but that is neither here or there. At that last supper they were eating and talking and just having a good time together, enjoying each other's company. It was not all fun and games though as the talks included who was going to betray Jesus. That had to be a little tense. I am reminded of John who is referred to as, "The one Jesus loved," and who leaned back against Jesus at the last supper to ask who was going to betray Him. He leaned back on Jesus—how cool is that? The time with Jesus seemed to be intimate times where all things hard and easy, fun and maybe not so fun, but important, were discussed.

It just seems to me that there is a special bonding that happens when we get together, share a meal, and spend quality time together and the meal seems to be an important part of that.

Remember after Jesus rose from the dead and was on the shore while Peter, Thomas, Nathanael, James, John, and two other disciples were out fishing? What did Jesus do for them? Well, besides telling them to move their nets to the other side of the boat and loading them up with a great catch after a long night of catching "nada," when they got to shore, He had made them a meal of fish and bread over a fire of burning coals. And don't forget about the feeding of the 5000 and then later on 4000 more, brought on by Jesus' compassion for the hunger of the people who had followed Him. Come to think of it, Jesus even healed Peter's mother in-law who had a fever and she immediately got up and made them a meal. How convenient. Wow, I feel so much better now that pesky fever has left me. Thanks Jesus. Is there anything I can do for You for healing me? Hmm. I know what you are thinking, "Please make me a lamb sandwich." Yes, I caught you.

A 30-Day Devotional

There is just something about this food thing. Women must instinctively know this because there is that saying that says, "The way to a man's heart is through his stomach." Interesting stuff I am writing here. I even have my own attention now. I could go on but all this food talk is making me a little hungry and my stomach is beginning to growl.

My point is this. In this verse in Revelation, Jesus is saying if we will let Him, He will come in and spend time with us. He does not say if we crack the door, He will push it open and fight His way in or put His foot through so we can't close it again. But rather, if we are willing, if we (not Him), open the door, Jesus himself will come in and sit down with us and share an intimate, personal time with us just like the pictures painted in the stories throughout scripture. So this same Jesus that John leaned on at the last supper is the same Jesus that is standing at our heart's door and knocking in this verse in Revelation. And I think that Jesus knocks a lot. He may figuratively have calluses on His knuckles for all we know. The first knock is to initially accept Him into our lives. But then there are further knocks—more personal knocks on doors of our heart that we don't necessarily want to open up to Him. You know, the doors to the places that we don't like many people to see. You know, where the real "US" lives, behind all the fronts and faces and masks. It started with the fig leaf and we have been hiding ever since. But we really can't hide from God. We just think we can.

In my life, it looks and sounds something like this: Jesus makes a slight fist and knocks on my heart door. No response is heard so after about ten seconds, He knocks again, this time a little louder. Inside David kicks his left little piggy toe hard into the foot of the heart couch and is now hopping on one leg while trying to peek out the blinds to see who it is. It is all he can do to keep in the pain his pinky toe is giving him, but somehow he manages. Then he hears Jesus knock again and say, "David? David?" At this, David dives behind the heart couch with a loud thud. Jesus continues, "David, I know you are in there, I saw you

Knock, Knock... Who's There?

peek out the blinds and heard your fat belly bounce off the floor when you dove behind the heart couch." David's brain is racing a million miles an hour for a proper response. In a flash of brilliance, it comes to him.

Slowly up from over the back of the couch rises a sock hand puppet and it turns its little white head toward the door. In a high, shrilly voice the puppet says, "I'm sorry Mr. Jesus, David is not here right now." "Where did he go?" Jesus asks with a grin. "I think he went to the store to buys some raspberry yogurt, four AA batteries, and some buttermilk," sock hand puppet responds. "Reeeaaaalllly? How strange. David does not even like buttermilk," Jesus says. "The buttermilk is for me, Mr. Jesus," hand puppet says. At this, Jesus walks away with a little smile on His face, knowing He will be back again soon enough and that one day, I will respond.

As silly as this example is, I think it represents the truth and our excuses are just as ridiculous. Jesus longs to have a deep and personal relationship with us, but He will not force it. And if we do accomplish this, then Jesus will want to have a DEEPER and MORE personal relationship with us. This process will continue again and again because we don't really know how to give everything we have to Him all at once. Each door He knocks on represents an even closer relationship with Him, trusting Him more. And more importantly, trusting us less. It may not be like this for everyone, but for me, it has been and will continue to be a life-long process. I think that Jesus will be knocking on my doors as long as I am doing this thing we call, "life." I think it will continue until I am standing in His presence. Then and only then, will I be finished.

I believe Jesus is knocking on the doors of every heart in this world. I believe we all have the opportunity to move as close to Jesus as we desire. But it has to be a deliberate act of our free will. We have to choose and choose Him above all the other things that call out for our attention in this life. Jesus knocks and says,

"Can I come in?" We either say, "No" and choose to stay the way we are because change is so hard and involves so much risk or we say, "Yes, please come in" and choose to let Him come in and change us in ways that might be hard no doubt, uncomfortable at best, and push us to our limits for sure but will ultimately be for our best in the end. The question is not, "Is He knocking?" but rather, "Are we brave enough to open the door?"

I think I hear someone at the door. Oh, I think it's for you!!! Knock, knock . . . Knock, knock . . . Knock, knock.

Jesus, we have so much to learn and it seems like we have so little time and pay so little attention to the really important things in life. And yet You still pursue us like lost lambs from the flock. Even after all these years, there are so many areas of me that are still lost and in need of Your rescue. In fact, all of me fits into that category because without You, I am nothing. But with You, I am a child of God, pure and spotless because of what You did for me. Thank You . . . Thank You . . . Thank You for the great love that You have for me and that I clearly don't understand. Please give me the courage and strength to open all of my doors to You as You did not hesitate to give everything for me.

Love,

David

Revelation 3:20

Here I am! I stand at the door and knock. If anyone hears my voice and opens the door, I will come in and eat with that person, and they with me.

Can you hear God knocking on your door? What will happen if you open the door to Him whenever he knocks?

Day 24
Milking It

I do not drink regular cow's milk anymore. I started drinking almond milk many years ago and I am now totally used to the taste. I made the switch because I had read and "herd" a lot about dairy and some of the problems it can cause and how it may not be that great for my body. Some of the things I came across left me cow-ering in fear and in a bad moo-d. And so I made the switch. But as much as I am happy with the change, there is still one thing I do not enjoy . . . the price. Really, it just seems to me that it is udderly ridiculous to demand such a heifer price.

Almond milk is at least twice as expensive as cow's milk and since I like to spend my money wisely, I wanted to be able to justify this. My long-term health of course is a great reason on its own, but I was searching to see if there was some reason that their production had to be more expensive. As I thought of this . . . a few bovine thoughts immediately came to mind so I decided to take the bull by the horns and look into it further.

First off, milking an almond has to be extremely difficult at best. You may possibly have to go to a specialty school to master the art of almond milking which would include of course, the study of the anatomy of the almond to teach you the best way to get it done. Heck, I am not even sure how to tell the gender difference between a male and female almond at this point. Learning all that surely cannot be cheap. And that is just to get someone qualified to even begin the process of getting ready to milk an almond.

And then I am sure it takes a chunk of cash to get the USDA (United States Department of Almonds) certification and stamp of approval. I am not sure if we would need to include the FDA (Federal Department of Almonds) or not but everyone seems to want their cut of the money, that is for sure.

Then there is the initial investment in the equipment. That price must be high for all the tiny, specialized milking equipment . . . and then the tech knowledge and dexterity needed to even use it.

First, you must have the tiny milking tubes and the almond udder attachments. Can a human even put them on an almond or does it have to be done with sweet precision robots and great computer programming? I am sure that procedure is as difficult as docking the space stations together. It is very high tech for sure.

And as you know, almonds have no legs so there probably has to be special stools they lay them on with holes down the middle. This is probably similar to a massage table where your face looks through the table. Those cannot be cheap and think of how many you would need? Almonds are small for heaven's sake, so to get any quantity of milk flowing, you would need many set ups and a pit crew as quick as the Indy 500 guys to hit the quota required to turn a profit.

And who brings in the herd of almonds? They seem pretty stubborn. I keep some in my pantry and every morning, I have to get them out of their container myself and put them in the zip-lock baggy and then into my lunch box. Never once has even one jumped out on his/her own. If I kept a cow in my pantry, when

Milking It

I opened the door, the cow would surely walk out all on its own. I don't think the cow would get in the zip-lock baggy on its own but still, they would at least come out of the pantry.

After considering all that goes into the production of almond milk, it is my conclusion that the truth may actually be that they are not charging us nearly enough for this fine product.

As fun as this story is and as ridiculous as it seems, it is really not all just plain nuts. In fact, there may be a little bit of cream on the top if we just milk it a little. And yes, I am the perfect one to do that.

Sometimes in life, we can believe something or not believe something about how things work or don't work or how things are or are not (yes, I know . . . very specific). Then one day, we find out one little thing that changes everything. Maybe we did not quite understand the "whole" truth about that situation. Maybe we ended up only being 2 percent or perhaps only 1 percent correct about what we thought. Or maybe we were actually 100 percent fat free of the truth.

Sometimes things are just totally (sorry in advance) "pasteurized" and are just difficult for us to see. What we believed was not all that it was cracked up to be and all we know for sure, at this point, is that we were wrong.

Time, experience, and patience can change things so much. Yet, it seems we are prone to jump to conclusions and quick to judge.

What we believe right now is based on our perception at this point in our life. And our perception is formed out of things that can include "true," "sort of true" and "not true at all." If you look back over your life, I'll bet you can see this in action. Were there not times when you believed something in the past but now you don't hold the same view?

Now consider that the same thing could be said about today. We are so smart in hindsight. It's just too bad we couldn't see then what we can see now. But then I guess it would not be hindsight anymore . . . it would be more like "back to the future."

So to sum this all up . . . let us believe what we believe in all grace and humility. Let us extend grace and respect to everyone God puts in our path. Let us not have to insist on showing that we are right but rather insist on showing that we truly love with the love that we have been show. And most importantly, let us always point away from us and instead to the One who truly loves us all beyond what we can comprehend.

Father, we have so much to learn and yet we often think we have it all figured out. Papa, please teach me to be humble and meek and to seek to share Your love and grace above all else. Teach me to love like You.

Love,

David

1 Peter 5:5-6

In the same way, you who are younger, submit yourselves to your elders. All of you, clothe yourselves with humility toward one another, because, "God opposes the proud but shows favor to the humble." Humble yourselves, therefore, under God's mighty hand, that he may lift you up in due time.

Have you been making "loving others" more important than "being right"? In what ways does God treat us with love?

Day 25
Don't Be Alarmed

The time was 10:43 p.m. and I had been fast asleep since about 10:00. In fact, IF sugar plums truly dance in your head while you are sleeping, I am pretty sure there was a disco dance club with a crowd of sugar plums dancing in my head with lights moving to and fro and a big shiny ball sending little light spots in every direction. And yes, of course they were all dressed like John Travolta in "Saturday Night Fever" attire. If the Sandman truly does sprinkle sand in your eyes to bring on dreams and sleep, my eyes surely looked like a warm, inviting beach and I was laying on an oversized towel with 30 SPF sun block evenly distributed on my perfectly tanned skin while I soaked up sweet vitamin D and sipped some kind of icy foo-foo drink from a crazy straw. If the depth of my sleep was represented by the ocean . . . okay, okay, in case you have not got the point yet, I was deep, deep, asleep . . . out of it even . . . gone to the world . . . tee-totally . . . asleep.

Then it happened, my 85-decibel smoke detectors went off in my bedroom, triggering all five other smoke detectors to join it in awful six-part screaming harmony. In a flash, I was out of my bed and standing in the middle of the room in total darkness in a "fight or flight" stance. I don't even remember getting out of bed. One second I was sound asleep and in the next, I was just standing there, ready to pounce like a riled cat. I am confident there were several back flips and maybe a half twist that I am not remembering as I sprang from my bed to the floor, scoring perfect 10s from the judges. And there I stood, ready for action. Then it just stopped. As suddenly as it had started, they all went mute as if nothing had even happened. There were no apologies, no cards, no flowers—just silence. Yes, you are right, very much like the end of a bad relationship. Five seconds of screaming and then that blaringly loud silence.

With my heart still racing, I walked over to the light switch and turned on the lights. I opened my bedroom door and smelled for trouble as I made my way into each room, first upstairs and then downstairs. When I was done and had found nothing, I made my way back to my room and waiting bed. It had missed me and was glad I was back, and I was glad to be back. It is one thing to have the annoying chirp of a low battery in the middle of the night, but this five-second, full-out alarm was an animal of a different kind. It had been . . . well, alarming.

Thinking it was all over, I settled back into bed and my wife and I again went back to sleep—until 11:00 p.m. Yep, you guessed it! Off it went again for round two of the same story. This time I was even more concerned because I thought the smoke detector must be picking up something. So, I gave the house another once over (or maybe that would be a twice over), this time going into the garage where my furnace and water heater were. There were no signs of trouble there. Checking the thermostat, it was several degrees away from even triggering the furnace, so that made me feel better that the furnace was in the clear for sure. And with that, leaving my bedroom door open just in case

Don't Be Alarmed

there was something to smell later, I went back to bed and fell asleep—until 11:30 p.m., that is.

With this alarm, I was more annoyed than alarmed when it went off. After the five-second screeching song, I climbed up on top of our five-foot-high armoire so I could reach the detector on the vaulted ceiling. I twisted to dislodge it from its base, then unplugged the wires from the back of the unit and finally gutted it by removing the backup battery. With that, my detector made a few more beeps, each one fainter than the last, then it went silent. Since the bedroom alarm seemed to be the start of all alarms, I had a hunch it was the offender. Sure enough, my instincts paid off and silence reigned the rest of the night.

A couple days later, I ended up replacing all six wired and two battery-only alarms. I had noticed while I was replacing all the backup batteries that there was a molded message under the battery compartment that said, "Replace this unit no later than 2005." Since it was now many, many years after that, I figured it was probably time. In my defense, no class in school ever told me to read molded messages under batteries on things that are screwed to ceilings. Just sayin'.

Have you ever had a false alarm go off in your life? I believe that most people have a few installed. They were installed during hard times in our lives to protect us in the future . . . or at least we think they will. Maybe one was installed after a broken relationship or loss of a loved one or any number of hard things. The alarms I am speaking of are anything that make you react without thought, like a reflex in a defensive way and sometimes makes absolutely no sense at all. I think this can also be known as, "Pushing one's buttons."

We come by them because it is natural for us to try to protect ourselves from being hurt in the future by someone or something that has hurt us in the past or the present. That's right, we can be installing alarms this very day that will affect us in the future.

A 30-Day Devotional

The problem is that many alarms we have installed in the past were not designed for what we have now and alarms we install in the present will not fit any better in future situations.

Here is an example anyone that had been divorced or ended a long-term relationship can probably relate to. Often we will react in ways in a new relationship that are based off alarms installed during old ones. Certain things that happen will trigger this old relationship alarm that was installed because of something hurtful or traumatic that happened in the past, but now the alarm is going off on someone that is not that person or that situation. It just kind of goes off like a reflex, leaving the person in the new relationship scratching their head and wondering, "What in the world just happened and what was that all about?" I know I have been guilty of that one, a time or two . . . or three (who's counting?).

A more personal example would be alarms that were installed in me because of losing my son in a fire. Because of this, I am overly sensitive to anything that could possibly cause a fire. My wife, Denice, has had to endure my alarm "going off" because of random things I have deemed unsafe at the moment. Most of these things would be considered normal in a sane person's life, but because of my past, not with me. She has also had to deal with me not wanting to leave anything plugged in that does not need to be plugged in. This led to the following situation:

We had started attending a new church and had invited the pastor's family over for lunch right after church for the first time. My wife put our lunch in our crock pot, plugged it in, and went on getting ready for church. Unbeknownst to her, I went through the kitchen unplugging toasters and whatever, also unplugging the crock pot by mistake. In my defense, she did not say, "Hey, this is our lunch, do not unplug the crock pot."

You can imagine the tension when we got home with our newly met guests only to find that her crock pot lunch was as cold as when she left—almost like it was not plugged in. When she noticed it was NOT plugged in, she asked me if I had unplugged

Don't Be Alarmed

it. I copped up to my mistake immediately in great humility. I had to, my new friend was a pastor for heaven's sake, and it went against my hard rule: "Never lie when a pastor is in your kitchen waiting to eat lunch."

So with all eyes on me and me with a cute little grin, I volunteered to make a quick run to Albertson's and get a bunch of chicken and cool stuff to go along with it. Because it was picnic food now, it was decided we'd abandon the dining room table and instead, spread a blanket in the middle of the living room floor. We all sat on the blanket like we were off in some grassy park on a sunny day and ate our picnic lunch while watching for ants. That day was the start of a lasting relationship with that family that has stood till this day. So really, in this case, my weirdness actually did us a favor. But most of the time it does not work this way.

It is my observation in life that we need to examine closely all of the things that set us off, get on our nerves, and maybe even make us scream like an 85-decibel alarm. To live in authenticity and maybe even to live sanely, we need to live in the here and now instead of the back there and used to be, while putting our hope in what God has for our future.

I think it may be a little like what the apostle Paul was meaning when he said, "Forgetting what is behind and straining toward what is ahead" in Philippians 3:14. Not many things can be gained by holding on to the mistakes of the past or the old you. Nothing can be changed no matter how much we hold on to it. The best we can do is just learn from it all . . . the good, the bad, the beautiful, the not so beautiful.

I heard a saying last year that made me laugh but at the same time, is full of truth. "The only person whose troubles are truly behind him is a school bus driver." We all struggle with the past for sure, but we really don't have time to dwell there. There are plenty of other things to keep us busy, I have no doubt about that!

This is what I suggest for you and for me. First, we must acknowledge that just like the alarm in my bedroom, not all alarms signal real danger. With that powerful knowledge, we begin to sort and sift and identify what is real and what is not . . . what is useful and what should have been thrown away a long time ago. We CHOOSE to learn from it all, confronting and casting aside any condemnation that tries to tag along.

This is not easy and not something we do best on our own. But as children of God, we are never alone. We have a "Helper," the Holy Spirit, to comfort us, lead us, and guide us through all the junk in our lives. We also have trusted people in our lives that God has placed there for just such a time. With God's help and the help of the trusted ones, all real and necessary alarms we leave in place while the old, outdated, and useless alarms we begin to twist off and unplug. One important note: make sure we take out the back up batteries as we do not want to follow anything that has come back from the dead, except our Savior.

In summary, we begin to identify the false and bury it all with Christ and begin to live in the real freedom, grace, and newness we have been granted in Him.

Father, we get so hung up on so many things that really don't matter in this life. We follow our own wants and desires and end up making such a mess of things. At times, we are much like a kitten wrapped up in a ball of yarn when we make our way back to You. On our own, we just can't seem to find our way out of this mess to the freedom You made for us to live in. Daddy please help me . . . please cut me free from all that binds me and keeps me from all the great things You want and have waiting for me. Show me the way and teach me to hear and listen to "only" Your voice and lead me to that perfect place in You.

Love,

David

Don't Be Alarmed

Philippians 3:13-15

Brothers and sisters, I do not consider myself yet to have taken hold of it. But one thing I do: Forgetting what is behind and straining toward what is ahead, I press on toward the goal to win the prize for which God has called me heavenward in Christ Jesus.

Psalm 103:11-14

For as high as the heavens are above the earth, so great is his love for those who fear him; as far as the east is from the west, so far has he removed our transgressions from us. As a father has compassion on his children, so the Lord has compassion on those who fear him; for he knows how we are formed, he remembers that we are dust.

2 Corinthians 5:17

Therefore, if anyone is in Christ, the new creation has come: The old has gone, the new is here!

Romans 12:2

Do not conform to the pattern of this world, but be transformed by the renewing of your mind. Then you will be able to test and approve what God's will is—his good, pleasing and perfect will.

What alarms do you have from your past that are hindering your relationship with your spouse, your friends, or God?

Day 26
The Hubcaps of Life

This morning as I was driving into work, I came across a lone hubcap. It was lying in the middle of the parking lot. It was obvious that it had been run over many times as there were pieces of its former self laying all around it. Some of those pieces were the clips that are made to secure it to the rim, giving the tire that much nicer look.

As I drove by it and saw all the pieces there, it was obvious that it would never go back on a rim again. Sure, you could probably super glue or even duct tape it back on, but in no time at all, it would be off the rim again. As far as how it was designed to stay on the tire, its job was now over and the rim would need to move on down the road.

As I thought about that broken hubcap lying crunched in the road, my mind quickly connected it to many things in my life. I have "moved on" to many different things during my life, leaving the old behind.

I have moved from being a baby to a toddler and left behind my rattle and my baby talk. I have moved on from a toddler to a little kid and left behind my slobber and my dirty diapers. I moved on from a little kid to a teenager and left behind my baby teeth and my grade school. I moved on from being a teenager to a young man and left behind some of my sassy attitude and from knowing absolutely everything about everything. I moved on from being a young man to being an older man and left behind some pride and arrogance and replaced it with humility and grace.

When I hit 40, the mean birthday gifts began to come and it seemed I had left behind my youth, larger bladder, and vision that could read a menu. Now that I am past the 50 mark, I have matured into this old guy (or like I prefer to think of it . . . fine aged wine that wears clothes and sometimes, a baseball cap) with much to think about this life. I am striving now to purposely leave behind all the things that attempt to hold me down or hold me back and have no value to me or my loved ones. I want to fully take on all the things that bring me life, happiness, love, and joy and all that God has for me. I am trying to fill my heart's treasure chest with all the great and precious moments this life has given to me and cherish them for what they are—priceless. And yet, there is still more to come. At the closing of this very day, I will be one day older still.

Some may argue that I am still just a big kid and to some extent, aren't we all or wish we could be again? As my body has moved on and gotten older, the "me" that is looking out these eyeballs and running all the hardware still feels like a young man. I am beginning to think it will always be like that. If I live to 90, I think that I will still feel much the same inside, but that my body will just not cooperate with me as much, like I've seen evidence of now. It's kind of a strange thing.

Sometimes we naturally move on with things in our life, like aging, as we have no choice in the matter. That makes those moves easier, though we may not like it. But there are other kinds of moving on that come to mind.

Sometimes we move on from jobs and/or relationships. Sometimes these things are our choice and sometimes they are

The Hubcaps of Life

not. Nevertheless, just like that hubcap, they are taken from our life rim and we roll on without them. Sometimes that painful hubcap is the loss of a loved one. These are so hard and affect us in so many ways for such a long time. They are profound losses and they change us forever. My family has had more than its share of these hubcaps in the past few years. And like it or not, life continues to roll on.

If you are anything like I am, you are not overly excited about change. You want to have as much figured out as possible so you can see what's coming. But in writing that sentence, it is obvious to me, that kind of living requires very little faith at all. But it is still my natural human instinct to want to live that way.

But the problem is God is always asking us to let go of things. Not because He is mean and cruel, but because He loves us and wants the most for us.

Our Christian walk is meant to be a journey and a relationship and that requires us to constantly be growing, learning, and changing into what God wants us to be. And just like a butterfly, it seems we are always emerging from some cocoon into newness with God. We pop out of our cocoon, spread our beautiful new wings of what God has shown us and then our next transformation immediately begins.

If we are allowing God to grow us, we should be able to look back over our lives and see the evidence. If we examine our lives and we do not see any change, any signs of growth, it might be time for us to seriously reevaluate things, looking for what the problem is and what we might be holding on to. What if we were to look over pictures of ourselves growing up and in every one of the pictures we looked the same. We would scratch our heads and wonder what was up with that? We would know something was wrong. In the same way, it is true with our spiritual lives in God. We were made to be growing and if we are not, something is wrong.

A 30-Day Devotional

We need to come to the understanding that if God is asking us to let go of something, it is for our own good. He is waiting for us to let go of it so He can give us something better and more fitting for where He wants us to be. But if we have our iron grip on the change and growth He is trying to give us, we stunt our growth where we stand. Do you love your Abba Father? Do you have any idea just how much He loves you? If you do, just let go.

Oh Father, we get so weighed down at times with the things of this life. We take on things You never meant us to take on and carry things around You have freed us from long ago. Father, this moment, I give you permission to reveal to me all the hubcaps that don't go with this sweet ride you have given me ... all those things You have already freed me from. And further, I pray that Your Holy Spirit will be with me to give me the strength to "let go" and let You grow me once again.

Love,

David

Isaiah 43:18-19

"Forget the former things; do not dwell on the past. See, I am doing a new thing! Now it springs up; do you not perceive it? I am making a way in the wilderness and streams in the wasteland."

1 Corinthians 13:11

When I was a child, I talked like a child, I thought like a child, I reasoned like a child. When I became a man, I put the ways of childhood behind me.

The Hubcaps of Life

Matthew 9:16-17

"No one sews a patch of unshrunk cloth on an old garment, for the patch will pull away from the garment, making the tear worse. Neither do people pour new wine into old wineskins. If they do, the skins will burst; the wine will run out and the wineskins will be ruined. No, they pour new wine into new wineskins, and both are preserved."

Psalm 84:11

For the Lord God is a sun and shield; the Lord bestows favor and honor; no good thing does he withhold from those whose walk is blameless.

Psalm 34:10

The lions may grow weak and hungry, but those who seek the Lord lack no good thing.

What broken hubcaps in your life do you need to leave behind?

Day 27
Spider Defense

A few mornings ago, I got up to get ready for work like normal. But this was not to be a normal morning. As I walked into the bathroom and turned on the light, I immediately noticed a medium sized spider in my sink. Now I must have looked pretty hideous with my hair sticking straight up and my freshly slept on face because the spider immediately ran down the sink toward the drain. Though I could not hear anything, I am sure the spider was probably screaming as he went. When he reached the drain, he quickly tucked himself up underneath the upper side of the drain plug and immediately tried to wipe away what he had just seen from all eight eyes and purge the awful image from his memory. I had watched him run to his hiding place under the drain and I started thinking about my plan to capture him and get him outside.

Yes, I did say, "capture," him, not squish him or drown him. The past few years and the older I get, I have increasingly developed a respect for life—not just human life, but all life in whatever form I notice it in. I do my best not to kill anything that is alive if I can avoid it. It is not always possible, but I do my best to let things go on living "outside my house" if I can. Much to my wife, Denice's, dismay, this had led to me finding, capturing, and carrying many things out of our house over the years. It has also led to me talking to the plants in the garden, thanking them, and telling them what a great job they are doing as I pick the veggies they have given to me. But we won't talk about that for now lest someone get wind of it and send in the guys with the straightjackets.

I think my wife should just be thankful that we don't live in the jungle. I can easily imagine myself running through the house with lions, tigers, bears, giraffes, lemurs, cheetahs, laughing hyenas, pythons, wild boars, small rhinoceros, and more, while yelling for her to GET THE DOOR PLEASE. Yes, I think that my wife is thankful now that we live in the city and flies, spiders, earwigs, and an occasional wallaby is all she has had to put up with me saving. But this morning, it was going to be a spider.

While the spider continued to hide, I got a prescription bottle ready. No, no, I was not going to drug him and of course a tiny safari tranquilizer dart gun, though very cool, was out of the question. This bottle was empty and it was going to be my makeshift spider carrier, straight to the front yard for the catch-and-release mission. But first I had to get him to come out of his hiding place.

Seeing him still underneath the drain plug, I decided to just lower it a little bit to put pressure on the spider to come out. This could have backfired and made him go deeper in the drain, but it was my best shot. When I lowered the drain plug and the other side of the sink touched his backside, he immediately came out of the drain and up the sink. At that point, I lowered the drain plug all the way down so he could not return to his hiding place. I had a tissue paper in one hand and the prescription bottle in the other. I lowered the tissue paper onto the path the spider was on and he walked right onto it. I lifted the tissue and moved the spider toward the bottle and went to put him in.

A funny thing happened as I was doing this. Maybe the spider thought I was going to squish him, maybe it was just a sweet

Spider Defense

circus trick he learned over summer vacation one year, or maybe it was just a God-given defense mechanism he had built in. But as I was putting him into the bottle, he rolled into a tight little ball and he just dropped to the bottom of the bottle and stayed there like that. To me, it was the equivalent of me getting into a fetal position, but what I really think he was doing was just playing dead.

There were no dramatics, no short or long goodbyes. He was just boom, "I'm dead, nothing to see here."

Maybe this spider had read in a sports magazine about how humans are taught, when caught by a bear, to play dead when the bear is thinking about eating them. Who knows for sure what was going on in this spider's mind, but this appeared to be his spider defense and stay alive plan for sure—play dead.

I have seen spiders do this before, but only for short periods of time and then pop back out and run away when they can. This is also when many have seen the bottom of a shoe. But this little guy was playing dead for all it was worth. While I took my shower, he continued to play dead. When I dried off and dressed, he continued to play dead. Finally, curiosity was starting to get the best of me and I was wondering if maybe he was actually really dead.

Maybe the excitement had been too much for him and he had a spider cardiac arrest. I would have no way of knowing. He had not complained about any pains in any of his leg, jaw, or chest. But I just had to know.

I opened up the prescription bottle and slowly rolled the spider out onto the tissue. He remained in the balled-up death pose ... until I went to put him back in the bottle. Then like a jack-in-the-box, he sprung to full size almost filling the bathroom counter and it was only because of my years of training and my working in the octopus packing plant during spring break that allowed me to get him back into the bottle. He had sprung open for his escape, but he had come up short. He almost had me fooled. All I can say is, "Well played, spider . . . well played."

When I was finally ready, I left the bathroom with the spider and brought him out front and released him back into the wild on my front lawn. He ran away quickly without a thank you, without a goodbye, and I knew then that he was going to be just fine. I only hoped that one day if I was about to be bitten by a spider buddy of his, that maybe he would remember me and return the favor by stepping in and stopping him. "That is the man that saved my life," he might be heard saying, as eight single tears ran down his spider cheeks from each of his eyes. A small tribute might break out in the spider world at that point, there's no way to know for sure.

Have you ever known anyone with the "spider defense?" What exactly am I talking about? I am talking about people who because of a situation they don't like or that is a little scary to them, their knee-jerk reaction is to first run and hide. And when they are forced to deal with the situation when someone lowers their drain plug and takes out their escape route, they shut down or play dead? And they play dead until they see an opportunity to spring back out and run away again? Sometimes during the escape, there are harsh reactions, designed to keep everyone away and to reset the boundary they think is keeping them safe.

And we are left to scratch our heads. After all, we were just trying to help them—set them free, so to speak. But you can't set someone free who does not want to be free. The choice has to be theirs alone. We also cannot expect those people to know that we were not there to treat them like everyone else has treated them their whole lives.

This world can be such a complicated place. We never really know what is going on in someone's head. We, or at least I, have a hard time keeping up with what goes on in my own head, much less, knowing why I think about the things I do. So we really don't know what someone else is thinking or why they think

Spider Defense

what they do. We do not know what brought them to this point in their lives and/or what all the pieces are that made them into the person we see.

Like I said, the world is complicated and people are complex. I am complex. I am an extreme peacemaker and I can drive myself crazy when there is an unresolved issue and someone is hiding from fixing it. I have learned the hard way that you can't force people to do something they don't want to do. They have the same freewill that I have, and they can choose the opposite of what I want them to do. And I just need to make sure that I keep my side of the street clean and then learn to deal with it. That is hard for me, but that is life.

So what do we do when we run into someone with the spider defense? Well, most people, in my story above would have just turned on the water, washed that spider down the drain and moved on with their day. And I think often we want to do that same type of thing with people like this. We judge them and flush them right down the drain and out of our lives and move on. And who can blame us? It's so much easier. But as Christians—people who have been loved unconditionally by our God—is this what we are called to do?

I think we can do better. If we can just understand that there is a story behind every person and a reason behind every action, maybe we can delay our judgment and perhaps dip into the well of compassion and mercy instead. Maybe we could try something different. Instead of flushing away things we don't understand because it is easier, we can just try to love people right where they are. Right in the middle of their hurt and dysfunction, right in the middle of their hiding, running away or lashing out. I mean really, isn't that what Jesus did and isn't that what He is still doing right now with you and with me? And if Jesus is doing it, aren't we called to do it also? Are we The Body of Christ or not? Something to think about. Are you with me?

A 30-Day Devotional

Father, I am failing. I do not love You or others in the way You love me. I do not forgive myself or others in the way that You forgive me. I do not believe in myself or in You in the way that You believe in me. Please change these things in me and my reconstruction will be well on its way. Please tear down what is holding me back and build up all that moves me closer to who You have made me to be. Thank You Great Lover of my soul.

Love,

David

James 1:19-20

My dear brothers and sisters, take note of this: Everyone should be quick to listen, slow to speak and slow to become angry, because human anger does not produce the righteousness that God desires.

Proverbs 15:1

A gentle answer turns away wrath, but a harsh word stirs up anger.

Is there someone in your life who had the spider defense that you need to reach out to and extend grace?

Day 28

Winging It

A couple of weeks ago, I was taking some things out to the trash. I went out just like I had a million times before. But as I was closing the lid to the trash can after placing my trash inside, I saw something out of the corner of my eye. This, "something" turned out to be a bird.

He was doing his best not to be seen by me and tried to walk away, which meant he was walking between me and the house.

As he walked by briskly saying things like, "nothing to see here," "move along," "hey, there is a sale at JCPenney's," I noticed that his right wing appeared to be messed up. It hung differently and the feathers around what would be the bird's armpit . . . or maybe in this case, the bird's wing pit, seemed to be severely ruffled. I made the deduction that it was probably broken or at best, dislocated.

I immediately felt compassion for my new-found feathered friend. He on the other hand did not return the affection and did not seem to be interested in my friendship. As I would move closer, he would walk away faster and try to put anything he could between him and me.

Now just to get the facts straight, this was not a sweet little sparrow. He was much bigger and some may have mistaken him for a pterodactyl or a condor. Others may have guessed an extremely large bald eagle or giant buzzard. But for the sake of this story and in case children are present, let's just say he was a little smaller than a medium size pigeon.

There we were, the bird making his way around the edge of the house and me crawling beside him. I was trying to figure out what to do. I wanted to help this bird, but I really had absolutely no idea how to do that. As a kid, I had helped baby birds that had fallen out of a nest, but they were easy. They just want food and don't run from you.

I had ideas of pouncing on him and putting him in my shed to at least keep him safe from the neighborhood cats but I thought that he might die of heart failure or I might die of heart failure if he started pecking me in the forehead. So I decided he had been through enough and threw out that idea.

I was probably out there for fifteen to twenty minutes trying to figure out what I should do. He was pretty much defenseless if a predator was to come across him, but no matter how sweet I talked to the bird, he would not let me come any closer than a couple of feet without panicking. And though he could walk fast, had a nice stride, and a smooth sway about him, it would not be enough to protect him. His feet were not the wings that God had given him to flee from trouble. But his feet were what he was down to now. And still he would not let me help.

Finally, after giving up the hope of him letting me pick him up, I retrieved a box from the garage and put it down near him so

Winging It

he would at least have some cover if he so chose. And then I left him to his own devices for the night.

I came out first thing the next morning and looked for him. I would like to tell you that he was safely in the box and wrapped up with a cute little bird blanket and lying on a bird pillow. But that would just make this a fairy tale, and this is no kid story. However, before you think the worst, I did not find him eaten or hurt or just a pile of feathers, I just did not find him at all. I followed the path he had been traveling the last time I saw him which led me down the side of the house and into the front yard. But I was never able to find him. I would like to think he made it somehow, but there is no way for me to know for sure.

Have you ever met someone like that bird? Maybe this person had been hurt in this life by someone or something or some circumstance beyond their control. Maybe the circumstance was even within their control, but still they were hurt. And though they use to fly around high as God made them to be, there they were now, grounded and barely making their way through this life. Their wing was broken or at best dislocated and their feathers had been severely ruffled by all that life had brought their way. And to make things worse, they trusted no one and would not let anyone get close enough to help them get better. And there you stood, ready and willing, but they would have none of it. Eventually you had to let them go on alone because of their choice, honoring the boundary they had set, like it or not.

More personal, at some point in your life, have you ever been that person, just trying to wing it and do your best to make it through another day? Maybe life had not played fair once again and you really just wanted to take your marbles and go home. But you could not find your marbles and you did not even know which way home was anymore.

I think most of us with some years behind us can relate in some way and say, yes, I have had a wing or two broken in this life. I know I have. I have been to that place a few times where I have been hurt so deeply that I did not ever think I could trust others again with that part of my heart. And so, I did what most people probably do. I gathered up those broken pieces and tucked them safe away from harm for years at a time. I have lost people in this life who went on living in this world and lost people in this life that have left me by leaving this world. Both hurt badly in their own way. On the flip side, I have also caused other people to feel the same pain and same way that I am describing.

After losing my almost one year old son in an accident and then steadily watching my second marriage crumble over time from the stress and grief of all that comes with that, I was a pretty broken man when it was all over. I was mad at God, mad at life, and really, just mad in general. I kept God at arm's length and anyone I dated at arm's length also. I wanted companionship, but only if the person could stay out of my safe zone. When they would cross that line and want more, I would panic, run and it would all be over in a flash. I know those women had no idea what even happened and it was not fair to them, but I was very broken and it was the best I could do at the time. I have heard the saying, "Hurt people, hurt people." I did just that during that time in my life. Every day we come in contact with people who are hurt in all kinds of ways, people who have been broken in this life for one reason or another.

So what can we learn from all this? One thing that comes to my mind right off is that there is almost always more to people than what we see on the surface. In my experience, nothing is really what it seems. The old saying, "You can't judge a book by its cover" is very true. I believe that there is a story behind every person—a reason behind every action. If we could somehow hear that story and know that reason, we might feel differently about them. The easy thing is to quickly judge them with what we see on the surface and then move on. But I think we are missing the mark miserably if we do this. The hard thing is to look at people like Jesus did.

Winging It

Two stories come to mind when I think of God's perspective on us: one is the prodigal son and the other is the woman caught in adultery.

In the first story, when the son has come to his senses and is coming home with only hopes of being one of his father's servants, his father sees him at a distance and begins to run to meet him. And upon reaching him, he throws his arms around him and pulls him so close. It seems to me that the father was waiting and longing for his son to return, for the day when he would again hold him in his arms. He was not waiting for him to come back so he could punish him and make him pay for all his stupidity and mistakes. He just wanted him to return home to him. His father restored him to his son status, not as a slave as the son was expecting. This is a beautiful picture of our Father's feelings for us when we have to do our own thing, have to do it our way and eventually our world comes crashing down. When we finally turn back to Him, we find our loving Father running to meet us—running to embrace us—running to restore us. Not because we deserve it, but simply because of the great love He has for us. God longs to be in relationship with us and went to great, painful, lengths to make it possible.

In the second story, we see a scene of a woman surrounded by people with stones in their raised hands as she cowers on the ground. We see her as guilty and worthy of death. We see this as justice. But judging by Jesus' response, He saw something very different. I think when He looked, He saw a woman who had sinned against His Father, surrounded by a lot of other people with stones in their raised hands, who were also just as guilty of sinning against His Father. People with hearts as hard as the rocks they held. And when He spoke that truth into that situation, "whoever is without sin, throw the first stone," one by one, rocks began to drop to the ground and people began to leave until it was just the woman and her Savior.

A 30-Day Devotional

Jesus saw someone in need of His love and forgiveness. Someone in need of a better way and another chance. Someone who simply needed to know Him. And Jesus simply loved her, just like He does you and me.

This last story speaks to my heart over and over as I walk through this life. It reminds me clearly again and again that without the love and sacrifice of Jesus and without His blood that was shed for me, I am only worthy of death. It reminds me of the great, unfathomable compassion and crazy, unimaginable love that our Creator has for us. If we could just see it.

Father, help me to see myself for who I really am—someone who is in desperate need of a Savior. Help me also to see all the people You put in my path as You see them. Please, please give me Your eyes and Your ears to see and hear people in the way that You do. Give me wisdom to see past the masks, the walls, the hurt, and the pain of the person that lies beneath it all. Father, please teach me to love like You.

Love,

David

Romans 3:22-24

This righteousness from God comes through faith in Jesus Christ to all who believe. There is no difference between Jew and Gentile, for all have sinned and fall short of the glory of God, and all are justified freely by his grace through the redemption that came by Christ Jesus.

Winging It

Ephesians 4:31-32

Get rid of all bitterness, rage and anger, brawling and slander, along with every form of malice. Be kind and compassionate to one another, forgiving each other, just as in Christ God forgave you.

Do you have compassion for hurt people that run away from help and love? Do you remember a time when you did the same?

Day 29

The Trouble With Stubble

Gravity is a very cool thing. You could even say it is "attractive." It is one of God's gifts He gave us to keep us grounded, so to speak. Without it, we would float off into space, which would make it very hard to do much of anything useful.

Gravity also has laws associated with it. When you are in the gravity zone, what comes up, must come down. You can believe in gravity or you can choose not to believe in it, either way, it's still there. Even though you can't see it, you are affected by it and can even test it if the mood strikes you.

Have you ever had someone say to you, "Go take a long walk on a short pier," or had your mom say, "If your friends jumped off a cliff, would you do it too?" If followed, both of these examples will demonstrate the law of gravity for you, whether you believe in it or not.

One day, long ago, the relationship between gravity, baldness, and nose and ear hair came to me in an epiphany.

I am an observer of life and I love watching it all around me. I try to see everything that goes by and around me or at least as much as I can. I learn the most from watching and observing and then by doing. I am a "hands on" kind of learner and life is a great teacher of great truth all around us. So now, back to my epiphany.

The startling thing I have noticed is that it seems like as most men get older, their hair begins to thin on top and sometimes even goes away. At the same time, as the hair gets thinner on top, the eyebrows get thicker and bushier and most distressing, hair begins to grow full throttle in their ears and their nose. Left untended, they can take over a face like weeds take over a garden.

I am convinced that a bald man at this stage could successfully grow out his eyebrows, comb them back over his head and if he used to wear bangs, no one would be the wiser until a wind from behind came along and flipped the brow rug. At that point, he would resemble "Cousin It" from the Addams Family. I think you might be beginning to see where I am going here. Don't run away, it's going to be okay.

This is my theory and I am sticking with it. I believe all I am talking about here is a direct result of gravity. Let me explain further.

As younger men, our bodies are stronger and fight this gravitational pull thing for as long as it can. But over time, the body grows weaker and must start to make choices concerning what it will fully support and what it will not. And one day, the body says, "I'm giving her all she's got, Captain!" and then hard choices are made.

At first, it gives up ground on the top of the head. The problem with this is that those hair follicles are not killed in the surrender and takeover but rather, they are just kicked out and sent packing if you will or even if you won't. They wander around like Moses and the people of Israel in the dessert until they settle just a little bit lower. Yes, it's true. And hair follicles must do what God designed them to do—grow hair. They have found

The Trouble With Stubble

their promise land and they begin to be fruitful and multiply. One day you get up and look in the mirror and say, "What in the world is that growing out of there?" as they begin to appear in the eyebrows, nose and ears—all the places you use to make fun of old guys for having hair. Yes, maybe a little bit of reaping and sowing at work here.

I believe that if we lived long enough, this migration would continue to move south and we would have periods of more and more upper body baldness and more and more lower body furriness. (Somewhere in this descent may explain the "soul patch" I see so many gentlemen wearing under their lower lip these days.)

At one point later in this process, there may be a stage that from a distance, we may look like we are wearing long pants at all times, as the landscape gets smaller and smaller for all the southward moving follicles to settle, live and grow.

In the very latest of stages, if we lived as long as some of the early people in the Bible, I believe we would have no body hair at all except for a huge bush like thing growing on our big toes.

I cannot back this up with any Biblical proof, but it is my opinion that this is one of the main reasons God decided to shorten the years that we live on this earth. Not because He did not see the bushy toe thing coming, but rather because of all the complaints He got from man because at that advanced age, it is very difficult to comb, brush out, blow dry, or perm your toe hair.

Now I love gadgets and I have a little story related to this subject to share with you. When the above gravity effect began happening to yours truly, I did not want to go down without a fight. Plus, kids tease you over anything in 4th grade and I was not going to give them any material. Anyway, I really did not like the idea of all that, "extra" growth and so I have fought it tooth and nail . . . or maybe in this case I should say, "I fought it brow, nose, and ear."

A 30-Day Devotional

In my ongoing battle, I found a thing called a "rotary nose hair trimmer." Sounds cool for sure and plucking nose hair is a painful and eye watering event. So I got one and I tried it.

I must say, I was very impressed with the first use of my "rotary nose hair trimmer." (RNHT going forward and just to be cool.) It surely lived up to all the hype and testimonies. I turned it on and sent it into the forest for a test drive.

An epic battle began immediately. RNHT against nose hair. Nose hair against RNHT. The noise seemed to be amplified because it was inside my head and it sounded like a cross between one of those tree limb grinders the tree trimming people throw their scraps into and a ninja tour guide with two machete's and a Swiss Army Knife carving a path through the deep, thick jungle.

In the end . . . the nose hair was the loser. My nose was clear and light crept into places it had not visited in some time. "Hello my old friend," I overheard it say. I had found a gadget that would be a new part of my arsenal and I was happy.

I was happy for about 24 hours. Then unexpectedly, something strange happened. I got a tissue to blow my nose and when I squeezed my nose together, there was a sharp pain. I was like, "Ouch!" and wondered what was happening. I squeezed again and it was more of the same. I immediately picked up the phone and called my wife, Denice, and yelled into the phone, "I HAVE NOSE STUBBLE!!!"

Oh, it was true. What was going on in my nose felt like a cross between an inward facing ring of sword drawn musketeers poking across randomly at each other and a litter of baby cactus taking up residence in my nose. Those little guys were not giving up so easily. I listened carefully and heard one of them yell, "Men, we may have lost this battle but we have NOT lost the war!" So it was with those mighty nose hair warriors (MNHW) and so it is with you and me.

The Trouble With Stubble

In my experience, life "rarely" works out like what we plan. We face a lot of situations in this life that seem good at first but often in the end, don't turn out like we thought they would. On the flip side, we face a lot of situations that appear bad or at least not very fun in the beginning but in the end, turn out much better than we anticipated. We have times of great celebrations and times of great disappointments. We have huge victories and disastrous defeats. It seems life is lived in a great spectrum, with periods where there may be only a nuance of change. But change is always on the way.

But in it all, good, bad, and in between, we always have the opportunity to learn. We have the opportunity to look at what all situations are teaching us.

In the victories and good times, we can see where we are strong, where we have grown and gaze back on just how far we have come. But we must never forget where we have been and WHO has brought us where we are, lest we miss the lesson. We must also always remember that as long as we are on this earth, our fight will never be over. We must live with a purpose, stay focused, continue to move forward, and continue to grow.

In the defeats and hard times, we learn who we are and we learn who we are not. Most importantly, we learn how to improve. We can identify where we need work and what we need to do to grow stronger. We learn not to cut some things short and not to let other things grow too long. Sometimes we learn just to leave certain things alone entirely. And in the midst of it all, we learn, like Goldilocks, what is "just right." We learn what works the best for us as we live, love, and mature into someone closer to who God is molding us to be.

And through the whole journey, we must not forget that, just like gravity, God is there walking right along with us whether we believe it or not. Even when life presents us with a lot of hairy situations or in times where we are taken right down to our roots—God is still there. He has plans and a purpose for us and He can use all that we experience and make them work out for His best and our best.

In this thing we call "our lives" and in this thing called, "the Christian Walk" we have an advantage—we already know how the story ends. Where we are now is not "it." When the "now" ends, things are really just beginning.

I heard this concept a while back and it stuck with me: "We are living in the land of the dying and moving toward the land of the living, not the other way around." Let that truth sink in. Even when things don't work out as planned "now," we know what is going to happen in the "then" (that place where there will be no more sorrow, crying, and death). That place where as Christians, we will live in eternity with the One that loved and loves us the most. How exciting, I can't wait. Until then, remember these words, "We may lose a battle here and there, but we WILL NOT lose the war."

Father, what an experience this life that You have given us can be. In our humanness, it is so easy to get lost in it all and at times, lose hope along the way. That is why we need your help so desperately and why I am asking You again and always to keep me so close to You. Daddy, please fill our hearts now with Your hope, Your love, and Your joy. Lead us and guide us in Your way everlasting and keep us in Your shadow and closely under Your care as we walk this journey before us.

Love,

David

Jeremiah 29:11-13

For I know the plans I have for you," declares the Lord, "plans to prosper you and not to harm you, plans to give you hope and a future. Then you will call on me and come and pray to me, and I will listen to you. You will seek me and find me when you seek me with all your heart.

Revelation 21:3-4

And I heard a loud voice from the throne saying, "Look! God's dwelling place is now among the people, and he will dwell with them. They will be his people, and God himself will be with them and be their God. 'He will wipe every tear from their eyes. There will be no more death' or mourning or crying or pain, for the old order of things has passed away."

Psalm 23:1-4

The Lord is my shepherd, I lack nothing. He makes me lie down in green pastures, he leads me beside quiet waters, he refreshes my soul. He guides me along the right paths for his name's sake. Even though I walk through the darkest valley, I will fear no evil, for you are with me; your rod and your staff, they comfort me.

Psalm 91:1-2

Whoever dwells in the shelter of the Most High will rest in the shadow of the Almighty. I will say of the Lord, "He is my refuge and my fortress, my God, in whom I trust."

How can you keep your eyes on what is to come—heaven?

Day 30

Twelve Horned Toads, One Mean Lizard, and an Earthquake

On February 9, 1971, my family and I lived in Sylmar, California. In one more month and two days, I would turn one decade old and life was good. But that morning at 6 a.m., I was awakened to the shakin' (sounds like a nice start to my first rap song) that I thought was my mom trying to wake  me up for school. I did not wake up immediately but opened my eyes when I heard the clunk of a toy car falling off my dresser. The drop to the floor somehow caused it to turn on and it began its journey across my bedroom floor. As I watched it roll on the carpet, my senses began to come to me and I realized that this was not mom shaking me, but rather, I was shaking along with everything else in the room.

I tried to get out of my bed but it was hard to stand. Slowly I made my way out of my room, up the hall, and toward my mom and dad's room. My dad was already up and in his bathroom. He was having problems opening the door because the house was shaking so violently and the doors were jammed.

When the shaking stopped, the doors were functional again and we all went outside. My older brother, Gary, was there with us as we made our way from the back to the front of the house through the field next door, because all of our cinder block fences had fallen. As we were going through the dirt field, my feet filled up with goat head stickers and I had to stop. Without missing a beat, my brother picked me up and carried me to the front of the house. He did not have any shoes on either and I'm sure he had just as many goat head stickers stuck in his feet that now were being pushed in farther because of my extra weight. But in that moment, he was much braver than I was and he was my rescuer.

With us all safe in our front yard, we soon learned that we had experience a 6.4 magnitude earthquake, centered not more than a couple miles from our location. Though there had been much bigger earthquakes, this one lasted about a minute and shook more up and down than side to side. Because of this motion, all of the "earthquake proof" freeway overpasses had come down. It also tore some of the wings off a nearby multiple floor "earthquake proof" hospital, leaving no walls and just beds showing for all to see. People were also trapped in underground parking and many did not make it out alive that day.

Because of the extensive damage to our house and many houses in the area, we lived outside in a small trailer for several months. We experienced many aftershocks and then new smaller earthquakes and I learned something—you never get used to the earth moving like that. It is always scary and it seems all your senses tell you to "RUN!" And off you go, having no real idea where you are going, but wow, are you making great time. It is a running motivator for sure and I am sure I could break a few world records in such a situation if I were competing.

Twelve Horned Toads, One Mean Lizard, and an Earthquake

One time, we were back in the house cleaning up. My brother had made it through the earthquake unscathed and rescued me from my thorny situation, but then two days later, he had stepped off the back step (yes, only one), twisted his ankle and sprained it quite badly. (Try getting into the emergency room two days after an earthquake.) So, now my brother was on crutches.

I was in the farthest bedroom from the nearest exit of the house, which was the front door. In between death and life is a long hallway with three bedrooms and a bathroom. There I was, minding my own business when another one of those pesky tremors hit. Just like all the rest of the times, I started running. As my brother would tell it later, he was also running—the best he could on crutches (that had to be a funny sight all on its own)—from one of those bedrooms. He was making his way down the long hallway when he was unexpectedly run over from behind and left for dead as he sprawled out in the middle of the hallway floor.

In my defense, to this day I have no recollection of seeing anything in the hallway, much less running up its back, over its head, and down the other side. And even though there were some suspicious sneaker tread prints in my size on his forehead, it doesn't prove a thing as they could have been left by any number of people running that day. I was simply doing what God had made me to do in that situation—run and scream like a little girl.

There was also another incident when my brother was being lowered down behind some cabinets that were pulled away from the wall. My dad was lowering him down, holding him by his feet. Guess what happened just then . . . yep, another tremor. My dad promptly let go of my brother's feet and ran out of the house, leaving him dangling upside down behind the cabinet to ride it out. I can just imagine the scene: screaming, thrashing, kicking of feet, a high-pitched voice yelling, "DAD???" I have to imagine the scene because I was obviously going to be found far from there, running and screaming like a little girl. What a trooper my brother was. Looking back, my dad might have remembered that as "getting the drop" on my brother. Yes, the life of adventure.

As we continued our journey of living in the camper, another fun thing happened.

There were still a lot of fields back in those days in the San Fernando Valley and that meant two things to me, lizards and horned toads. I always seemed to have a collection of one or the other and on a good day, both. At the time of the earthquake, I had 12 horned toads and one mean lizard. Six of the horned toads were full grown and six were cute little babies still in diapers and they all lived in an aquarium that had been their home for some time.

The lizard was a stubborn one. He was very big and was not one that I had caught in the wild wilderness, but rather one that a friend of my parents had bought me for a present of some sort. I think he was called an "alligator lizard" and for good reason. I learned quickly never to take a bath with him. The horned toads were pretty tame and I would pick them up and turn them on their backs and rub their bellies which would put them to sleep. Or maybe it was making them pass out, but from my child perspective, their eyes were closed so they were asleep. But this lizard would have none of this kind of treatment. He was fierce and would try to bite me every chance he got. Luckily, he did not have much of anything to call teeth or I would probably have been fingerless before puberty and unable to type this now. There was just no taming this vicious lizard. He was mean, sassy, and full of spit and vinegar. His language was pretty edgy also and with his accent, it was all I could do sometimes not to throw down with him from time to time.

On one hot day, for some reason that I don't remember, I needed to get the reptiles out of the sun. Maybe I was out of sunscreen for them or maybe one had lost his little sunglasses, but all I know for sure is that they needed shade. Being the brilliant child

Twelve Horned Toads, One Mean Lizard, and an Earthquake

that I was, I put the aquarium in the only obvious place that most people of good judgment would choose. Yes, under the back of my dad's car behind one of the tires. Wow, I was hoping that writing that down would make this sound better somehow, but it does not.

How many of you would like to guess what happened next? Yes, I see your hands, brothers and sisters. As you have all guessed, my absent-minded dad went and decided to back his car out of the driveway without checking with me first to see if I had maybe put an aquarium with 12 horned toads and 1 mean lizard under his car behind his back tire. I know, I know, parents are not perfect.

After he heard the crack, he stopped the car and gazed upon what must have looked like a terrible scene from a driver's education film he had once watched in high school. You remember the one about what can happen if you fail to ask your children if they have put any of their pets behind your back tire before backing out of a driveway.

When I was called to the scene, I was expecting the worst, some very flat horned toads and my mean lizard still biting the tire. But what I found was shatter glass, small beads of gravel, and all 12 horned toads. The mean lizard was of course long gone and probably halfway to the border by now. But all my horned toads were still there. They were doing their horned toad thing in their horned toad way, all just sitting there in the remains of their aquarium with glass shards all around them not even realizing that they were free. And so it is with you and me.

Have you ever woken up one day only to find your reality shaken to its very core? Have you ever been faced with the fact that everything you thought was solid and unmovable in your life, was really just an illusion of stability and security? You would have bet your life that these things could not and would not ever change. But then, much to your dismay, one day they came crumbling down to the ground like a freeway overpass or a wing torn from hospital, leaving you completely devastated, vulnerable, and exposed to everyone it seemed.

Life has a way of doing this to most of us. Could it be that "Someone" is telling us that we are not to put our security in things on this earth and the ways of man, but rather in something bigger—much, much bigger? To trust the One that made everything we know, every good thing we see and even you and me—the very One that knows absolutely everything about us and that knit us together in our mother's womb—the all-powerful, loving One that knows what we are going to say before the words even reach our tongue and who wrote about all the days of our lives in His book before even the first one started? Yes, it could be.

I believe everything that happens to us is at least allowed by God, if not sometimes sent by God to help us in the long run. We may not see it at the time or even like it much, but it is still the truth whether we like it or not. When the mean teacher gave us a test in school, it showed us what we knew and what we did not know (mostly what we did not know in my case). Every test we are given by God is sent with design and purpose in mind and we have the opportunity to learn from it if we choose to or take the class over again. I have taken many classes over and over and over again and I do not recommend it.

Sometimes God smashes our reality to free us from something in our life. But instead of seeing the gift and opportunity He has given us, sometimes we miss it and focus on what we had and lost, instead of what is now and what could be. We stay there and live among the shards of broken glass, sometimes even trying to glue the pieces back together. Not unlike my 12 horned toads, we were freed and don't even know it. God sighs and the devil dances.

Sometimes God frees us and calls us to something bigger and much better than where we have been living. He calls us to something more than just how we have always done it, the way that has kept us unsuccessful or at best limited for so long. And

Twelve Horned Toads, One Mean Lizard, and an Earthquake

sometimes He just jumps in the car, backs it up, and shatters our small aquarium view of life and simply says, "Now walk away and just follow Me." And then He waits.

My Father, how often have I missed what You have tried to show me in my life? How patient You must have had to be with this distracted and short-sighted student and son. I thank You so much for Your loving kindness and great love and for never giving up on me. I thank You for loving me enough to shake up my world, for tearing down my overpasses and ripping off my wings from time to time and for running over my aquarium when I need a perspective change. Thank You so much for being such a great Daddy.

Love,

David

Isaiah 43:18-19

"Forget the former things; do not dwell on the past. See, I am doing a new thing! Now it springs up; do you not perceive it? I am making a way in the wilderness and streams in the wasteland."

When has God shattered the box holding you and given you freedom to follow Him? Have you seen that your past is gone and your future secure?

Acknowledgments

I would like to thank my wife, Denice, for all of her support and for believing that I had something valuable to share with people. Thank you for being willing to allow me to invest my time, energy, and money into this project and others. Thanks for believing!

I would like to express my gratitude to Aloha Publishing. Your team is fantastic. You are so supportive and creative and I have been humbled and honored to work with all of you. I hope you are a part of all my future books.

Lastly, I would like to thank all the people who have laughed at my crazy sense of humor and my different takes on life over the years. I would also like to thank the ones who refused to laugh, but I knew you were laughing on the inside anyway. You all encouraged me to continue to share a little of what goes on in this crazy head of mine.

About the Author

David L. Wood is a husband, father, author, singer, songwriter, and worship leader in the Pacific Northwest. The hope in his stories will spark thoughts about God's constant involvement and intervention in our lives. His writing stirs a sense of how much God cares about every detail that is important to us. He sings and teaches on grace, grief, and the hope of Jesus. His humor and sincerity is felt in his books and songs. David is married to Denice and is the proud father of six beautiful daughters and is "Papa Dave" to twelve grandchildren.